Considering Conservation

Energy, Power Sources and Electricity

Philip Neal

Dryad Press London

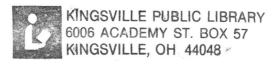

Contents

Acknowledgments

The author would like to thank the following for their help in the preparation of this book: Ian Cain (Ecotec Research & Consulting Ltd); Centre for Alternative Technology; Chronar Ltd; H. Eccles (British Nuclear Fuels); French Embassy; Suzanne Grundstrom (Solar Energy Research Institute, Colorado, USA); Dominique Guerin (Chambre de Commerce et d'Industrie, St Malo); Dr Hay (Nottingham University); Ian Jarvis (Leicester County Council); Mary Jean Johnson, Salt Lake City, USA T. E. Langford (CEGB, Marchwood Engineering Laboratories); I. D. Mays (VAWT Ltd); Rita Neal; I. D. Parker (Midlands Branch CHPA); Purfleet Board Mills; Maggie Thompson (Warmer Campaign); A. M. Townsend (Oxford Forestry Institute); US Department of Energy, Maryland, USA; Walt Disney World, Epcot Centre, USA.

For help and providing illustrations AGA Thermovision *cover*; Anthony Biddle and Liz Genders (PEEL Ltd) 43; Associated Press 13 *bottom*, 16; Neil Boise (Newfoundland University) 29 *bottom right*; Malcolm Cowling (Ruston Gas Turbines Ltd) 42; David Gilmour (James Howden) 28 *bottom, front cover* top; K. M. Groechel (McAlpine VAWT) 29 *top left*; D. A. Hall (MEB) 16; Sandra Hobbis (British Brown-Boverie Ltd) 17; Lesley Munnoch (BP Solar International) 20 *centre*; R. H. Parker (Geothermal Energy project) 26 *bottom right*; Henry Rosenbluth Albuquerque, USA 26, 27; Pat Stephens (Princeton University Plasma Physics Laboratory, USA) 7; Terraset School, Reston, USA, Principal, Staff and Pupils 22 *top left*; Claire Trevor (UNEP) 15; P. B. Williams (Laing ETE) 37. For illustrations Associated Press 11, 14; B. T. Batsford Ltd 2; Carol Chapman 43; Electricity Council *diagram* 12; Energy Efficiency Office *diagram* 4; 20 *top*; Bob Jones and B. Rose (CEGB Stockport) 31 and *diagram*; Kjell Løvaas (Norwave, Oslo) 32 *bottom right*, 33; Needham Chalks Ltd 39; Christine Phillips 18 *bottom right*; Sandia National Laboratories, New Mexico, USA 20 *bottom*; Weatherwarm Home Insulation Ltd *diagram* 12. The line drawings on pages 1, 2, 4, 6, 8, 9, 13, 15, 16, 17, 21, 33, 36, 37, 38, 39, 40, 43, 44, 47 *cover* are by Sue Prince. All other photographs and illustrations are the authors.

Cover illustrations

Top: Wind farm, Altamont Pass, California, USA. There are 75 330KW turbines and 1 750KW turbine. (James Howden & Co.)
Centre: A heat loss (thermovision) picture of semi-detached houses. On the right the actual houses. On the left a heat loss picture of the same houses. The greatest heat loss is coloured red, then in descending order, light blue, purple, green, with dark blue showing the least heat loss. Notice how most heat is lost through the windows and how the outside tiling and wooden boarding prevent loss of warmth. Even the gutter downpipe prevents heat loss. (Agema Infra Red Systems)
Bottom right: Sunset at Kanoni, Corfu. (Philip Neal)
Bottom left: The overhead electricity grid system. (Sue Prince)
Title page: Dounreay nuclear power station. (Philip Neal)

© Philip Neal 1989
First published 1989, 1991

Typeset by Latimer Trend & Company Ltd, Plymouth and printed by Courier International Ltd, Tiptree, Essex. For The Publishers
Dryad Press, 4 Fitzhardinge Street, London W1H 0AH.

ISBN 0 85219 776 4

Introduction

Burn a piece of *coal*: it gives out heat. The coal is gone for ever. Burn a piece of *wood*: it gives out heat. The wood is gone for ever. The two cases are the same ... or are they?

The coal has taken millions of years to form. It was once part of a tree. It was buried deep underground, where pressure, time and heat caused it to change from the wood it was, to the black shiny material it is today. There is still much more coal to be mined, but no more can be created during the small amount of time we each live on earth. We say that coal is a FINITE resource: once used, it cannot be replaced.

The wood we burn has taken from a few years to a few hundred years to grow. It was part of a tree as well, perhaps part of a branch that was blown down or sawn off. It may have been part of a tree that was totally felled. Whichever is the case, a new tree can be planted or a new branch will grow. Though the actual piece of burnt wood has gone for ever, it can be replaced by other growth.

The coal is called a FOSSIL FUEL energy source because, like fossils, it has taken ages to form. The wood is called a RENEWABLE energy source, as it can be replaced.

Energy sources like coal and wood can be used to create electricity – which is a convenient way of moving energy from one place to another, from where it is made to where it is to be used. This book is about how power in the world is used to create energy, and particularly electric energy. Although it will describe the most common ways for making electricity, it is mainly about trying to create energy from sources which can go on always because they, like wood, are renewable. It is also about CONSERVING energy and not wasting this valuable resource.

So what is ENERGY?

The US space shuttle Discovery *above the world with its 32 m (105 ft) solar power collector extended. The array of 84 panels of solar cells produces 12.3 KW of electricity.*

Dictionary definitions

What definitions of ENERGY are given by the dictionaries? Here are parts from three of them:

Energy = "Force, vigour, active operation" (*Concise Oxford*).

Energy = "The capacity to do work and overcome resistance" (*Webster's New World*).

Energy = "The power by which anything acts effectively to move or change other things. ... The capacity of doing work and of overcoming inertia, as by heat, light, radiation, or mechanical and chemical forces" (*Encyclopaedia Britannica*)

Energy

Albert Einstein
He was born on March 14th, 1879, at Ulm in Germany, to a Jewish family. During his life he resided in Italy, Switzerland (where he failed the entrance examination to Zurich Polytechnic!), Germany (Berlin), Paris and for the last 22 years in the USA, working at Princeton University. He died on April 18th, 1955, at Princeton. He has been called the most famous scientist of the twentieth century, perhaps the greatest genius of all time.

Sometimes a person lives who reveals an important truth about the way the world works. Archimedes, Newton, Marie Curie, Marconi, Rutherford; I hope that you have heard of these people and know what they discovered (see end of page 5). What about Albert Einstein? Do you know about him?

He was a mathematician and he put forward the LAW OF RELATIVITY. In it he said that the universe is made up of MATTER (gas, liquid, solid) and ENERGY. MATTER can be turned into ENERGY. ENERGY can be turned into MATTER. The amount of ENERGY and MATTER added together is always the same – no more can be created and none can be destroyed. ENERGY is a force which can make MATTER move. This movement can be harnessed to provide power for work.

> **Measuring energy and power**
> How do we measure energy and power? You may have heard of *horsepower* as a measurement of the energy produced by a car engine, and of *watts* as a measurement of light energy. However, the basic measurements of energy are in *British Thermal Units*, or, now that we are increasingly metricated, in *Calories*. This is not the book for detailing all about measuring energy, so I will only briefly explain to you that:
>
> *1 British Thermal Unit* (BTU) is the heat required to raise the temperature of 1 pound of water by 1 degree Fahrenheit (1 lb by 1°F).
>
> *1 Calorie* is the amount of heat required to raise the temperature of 1 gramme of water by 1 degree Centigrade (1 gm by 1°C).
>
> To give you one example, 36 litres (8 gallons) of petrol has the energy to produce 1 million BTUs
>
> 99% of our energy comes from the SUN, as we shall see on page 6.

Water in a lavatory cistern is an energy source waiting to be used. When the chain (or handle) is pulled, the water rushes down the pipe and uses its power to flush the toilet bowl.

Power of falling water stored ready for use

Potential Energy

There are two sorts of ENERGY:

1 KINETIC, which is energy in action.
2 POTENTIAL which is energy waiting to be used, energy in reserve.

Kinetic energy can be changed into potential energy and vice versa.

Kinetic Energy

Power of human muscle used directly

Human muscles can be used to provide direct power. The energy comes from the food we eat. When the car engine is working, the power is coming from oil (as petrol), a fossil fuel.

4

Let us think of the different ways in which we provide power to make energy.

Types of power

Pushing a car needs muscle power. Many people use their muscles on a piece of equipment which is designed to make human muscles more effective: a bicycle for example. Leg muscles turn the pedals, which connect a large cog wheel to a smaller one. Together with bicycle wheels this makes the person speed along much faster than by using legs directly to walk or run.

Here is a list of different types of power. On the right-hand side are two examples of machines or devices where each type of power is used to create energy. You can think of some more examples. Some of them will go against more than one type of power.

Type of power	Uses
Muscle	Pulley, Treadmill
Falling water	Hydro turbine,* waterwheel
Wind	Glider, yacht
Compression	Spring, pump
Spinning	Flywheel,* axle
Magnetism	Magnet, magnetic material
Electrical	Motor, vacuum cleaner
Heat	Heat exchanger,* steam engine
Chemical	Battery,* car engine
Mechanical	Gear, pendulum
Nuclear	Atomic reactor,* isotope
Electromagnetic	Lighting systems, heating

* to be explained later

Most uses involve several different forms of power. To make a bicycle work, muscle, spinning and mechanical power are all used. Where would you put "explosive", "elastic band", "lever" and "referee's whistle" in the list?

Heating, lighting – industry and communications

One of the most important uses of the world's power is to provide heat for warmth and cooking. For us, in the developed world, this probably means using electricity or gas. Not

Humans have trained animals to use their great muscle power for our use.

Food supplies our bodes with the energy we need to go on living. Originally the sun has provided the energy for the food itself.

One food calorie is the equivalent of 1,000 heat calories (one kilocalorie) or 3.97 BTU. Nowadays all food packets have to show details of their contents to indicate food values including energy.

TYPICAL NUTRITIONAL COMPOSITION PER 100g	
Energy	326k cals
	1360kJ
Protein (N × 5.7)	10.3g
Fat	1.1g
Dietary Fibre	15.5g
Available Carbohydrate	66.1g
Vitamin C	25.0mg
Niacin	15.0mg
Riboflavin B2	1.3mg
Thiamin B1	1.0mg
Vitamin D3	2.0μg
Iron	40.0mg

An average 30g serving of Bran Flakes will provide at least one quarter of the average adults recommended daily intake of the above vitamins and the full daily recommended amount of iron.

many of us nowadays actually burn solid fuel in an open fire. Nonetheless, fuel has been burnt in order to make our electricity. For many millions of people in Africa and Asia, burning some kind of fuel is still the main method of providing heat for warmth and cooking.

It is the same with light. Whether we burn a candle or switch on an electric light bulb, we are using power to create energy.

The gadgets we use in our homes and in our local neighbourhoods have had to be made – think of knives and forks, street signs, carpets or paving slabs. A great deal of power is used to create energy for manufacturing goods. In the developed world the manufacturing industries are sophisticated. Elsewhere in the world, making things is much simpler; it can be as basic as hollowing out a tree trunk to build a canoe.

Our last major use of power is probably to create energy for moving ourselves and our goods from one place to another. Cars, planes, trains, bicycles, rickshaws, sledges, lorries, boats, space rockets, wheelbarrows – you can make a list that is very long and which includes simple vehicles and elaborate technology. We could not accomplish much of our movement without moving words and pictures around as well. We call this communication and it includes radio, television, telephone and satellite. The simplest forms of communication are drum beats, smoke signals and reflected lights.

What did they discover?

Archimedes – volume; Newton – gravity; Marie Curie – X rays; Marconi – radio waves; Rutherford – splitting the atom.

How electricity is made

Power stations produce *heat*. The heat is used to turn water into steam in a *boiler*. The steam travels along pipes to the *turbine*. It hits the *turbine blades* and makes them spin. The spinning turbine drives the *generator* which produces electricity.

The steam then goes to a *condenser* where it turns back into water. The water returns to the boiler, where it is heated again to produce steam.

With hydro-power the falling water turns the turbine directly.

The electricity travels along cables to a *transformer*. The transformer changes the electricity from a low voltage to a high voltage. This is the best way to send electricity over long distances. The electricity travels along overhead *grid* lines to a *substation*. At the substation, a transformer changes the high voltage to a lower voltage. The electricity then passes along more cables to homes, schools, factories, and other users.

How a nuclear reactor works

In a nuclear reactor, heat is produced by the splitting, or *fission*, of the nuclei of atoms of materials such as plutonium and uranium. With uranium, the process also produces fast-moving particles called neutrons which can strike other atoms and cause them to split. Further neutrons are then produced which cause further fission

Electric power is carried by the grid system at 132,000 or 275,000 or 400,000 volts. It is transformed down to 240 volts into our homes. Electricity is produced by the Central Electricity Generating Board in England and Wales and by the Scottish EGB north of the border. The power is moved around the country by means of the centrally controlled grid system, well-known to us by its overhead power lines which carry the power at very high voltages.

Power lines and their pylons are very, very dangerous. Keep well away from them. Recent research has suggested that the magnetic fields set up by the electricity in the grid may harm the health of people living underneath.

Government proposals are in hand to change the organization of the Electricity Generating Boards and to place them into private rather than public ownership.

and so on. In a power-generating nuclear reactor, the number of neutrons available to cause further fission is regulated by control rods made of boron steel, a material which absorbs neutrons.

How electricity is made. *The percentage figures show the proportion of each kind of energy source in the UK in 1987.*

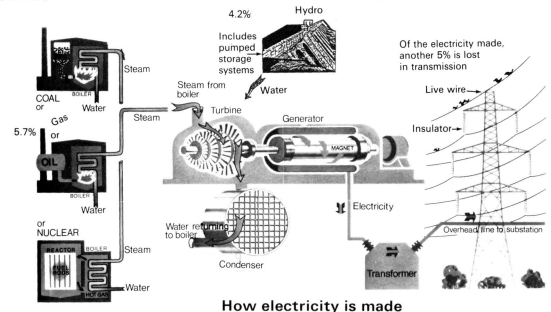

How electricity is made

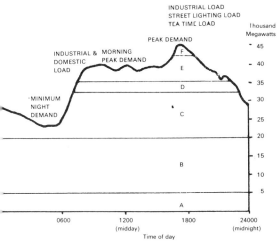

INDUSTRIAL LOAD
STREET LIGHTING LOAD
TEA TIME LOAD

PEAK DEMAND

INDUSTRIAL & MORNING
DOMESTIC PEAK DEMAND
LOAD

MINIMUM
NIGHT
DEMAND

Thousand Megawatts

Time of day

A typical weekday demand curve, and how the CEGB might meet the demand.

The electricity is drawn from these types of power station:

A Nuclear and hydro
B Modern coal-fired
C Older coal-fired
D Modern oil-fired
E Older oil-fired
F Pumped storage hydro

There is a steady demand for electricity all day long. At certain times there is an increased demand. These are PEAK TIMES. The CEGB uses its cheapest means of generating electricity first of all and brings in its more expensive power stations during peak hours. It uses its pumped storage stations to meet sudden demands, which sometimes occur, for a lot of energy. (See the Thorn Birds graph on page 33.)
(Source: CEGB)

In the fission process heat is produced. The reactor becomes hot and heat is extracted by a liquid or a gas which is pumped cautiously through the reactor core. This *coolant* is then passed through a heat exchanger, which is very like the boiler in a conventional power station.

Nuclear reactor power stations
There are several kinds of nuclear reactors in the UK:

MAGNOX (the oldest type)	The nuclear fuel is in Magnesium Alloy Cans. The coolant is Carbon Dioxide gas.
AGR (Advanced Gas-cooled Reactor)	This works at a higher temperature.
PWR (Pressurized Water Reactor)	The coolant is water but at such a high pressure that it does not boil.

The arguments for and against nuclear power stations

FOR Clean – no smoke
No lorries or trains bringing coal.
No ash.
Plenty of fuel.

AGAINST Danger of radiation – not confined to country owning power station.
Radioactive waste left – disposal difficult.
Some waste could be used for making bombs.

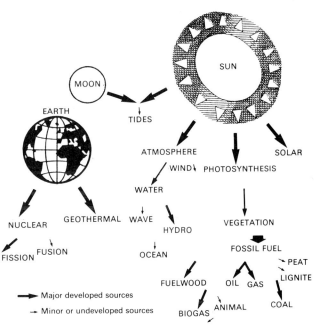

Energy flow and energy sources.

Question: Why can birds perch on the overhead power lines without receiving an electric shock? (See page 64).

Answer: They do not touch the ground, and so do not complete an electric circuit. **DO NOT EVER ATTEMPT TO IMITATE THIS.**

7

The sun – it keeps us going

Ninety-nine per cent – in other words, virtually all of the energy we have on earth – has come from the sun! The other 1 per cent comes from the internal heat of the earth and from the gravitational pull of the sun and the moon on our world. However, even that 99 per cent is only one thousand millionth (1/1,000,000,000th) of the heat energy produced by the sun. The sun is 93 million (93,000,000) miles from the earth, and yet human skin will be burnt if exposed to its rays for too long. This indicates the huge amount of heat that the sun produces. Some scientists say that the actual heat of the sun itself is equal to 400×10^{18} kilowatts of power (400 with 18 more 0s on the end). If you remember that a one-bar electric fire uses 1 kilowatt in one hour, that will give you some idea of the incredible heat of the sun. The amount of energy from the sun which reaches the earth is about the same as will be given out by *173 million* large electric power stations working at full production all day!

Unfortunately, as the diagram shows, even that small proportion of the sun's total energy which reaches our planet does not all become available to us.

The sun itself is a giant nuclear reactor. As far as scientists can discover, it works like this. Inside the sun heat reduces matter to an ionized gas called PLASMA. In this plasma atomic particles overcome their electrical repulsion which normally causes them to stay apart from each other. Instead they collide, join together (this is called FUSION), release energy and keep on doing this – scientists call it a self-sustaining process. Whereas nuclear fission splits atoms, nuclear fusion joins them together. In both cases there is a tremendous release of energy. (Fission is the process which causes ATOMIC BOMBS to explode. HYDROGEN BOMBS explode as a result of fusion.)

Energy from the sun.

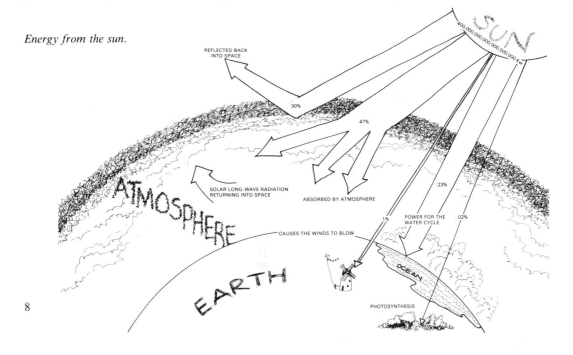

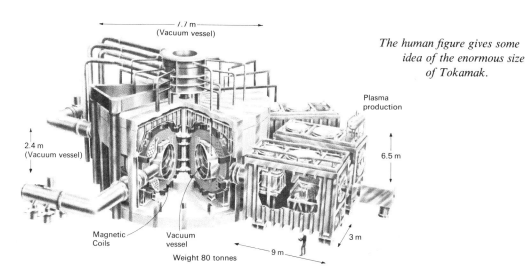

7.7 m
(Vacuum vessel)

The human figure gives some
idea of the enormous size
of Tokamak.

Plasma
production

2.4 m
(Vacuum vessel)

6.5 m

Magnetic
Coils

Vacuum
vessel

3 m

9 m

Weight 80 tonnes

A diagram of the Tokamak Fusion Test Reactor. *The reactor basically consists of apparatus to produce ionized plasma and inject it into a vacuum vessel surrounded by magnetic coils. The research target with TFTR is to confine an ionized gas of the heavy isotopes of Hydrogen, which are Deuterium and Tritium, at a temperature of 100 million°C, the physical condition needed to produce fusion energy. In July 1987 TFTR hit 200 million°C, the highest temperature ever made in a laboratory.*

At very high temperatures, atoms of hydrogen combine to form helium. Every second, in the sun, over 600 million tonnes of hydrogen are changed into slightly less helium, and enormous amounts of heat energy are released to earth. On earth this energy is used to form chemical bonds in plants, between hydrogen and carbon: this makes hydrocarbons. The fossil fuels, oil, gas and coal have been formed from plants. When they are burnt, the bonds of the hydrocarbons are broken and heat energy is released. Burning fuel is one way in which the power of the sun is transformed into energy.

Turning solar power into electricity is the main way of providing energy for the peoples of the world, particularly those in the developed world.

All things to do with the sun are enormously complex and scientists are finding out more and more about it, and about energy itself, as time passes. The most that the majority of us can do is to realize that our whole existence relies on the sun and its provision of energy. We should also remember in considering conservation, not to waste the energy that is provided. We must try to use those power sources which will not harm the people who will inhabit the earth after we have gone. We must seek the facts, decide what is best based on this evidence, and proceed from there.

Fusion energy experiments worldwide

HIGH TEMPERATURE

There are four main fusion energy experiments, which try to reproduce the power of the sun. They are known as Jet in Europe, JT 60 in Japan, T-15 in the USSR and TFTR (Tokamak Fusion Test Reactor) in the USA. Their aim is to prove that fusion power is possible without being too expensive to produce. On April 23rd, 1988, the USA, the USSR, Japan and the European Community agreed to produce an International Thermonuclear Experimental Reactor (ITER) by the end of 1990 – a fusion reactor.

LOW TEMPERATURE

On 22 March 1989 a claim was made by Professors Fleischmann (Southampton University) and Pons (Utah University, USA) that they had achieved Nuclear Fusion in a laboratory experiment without using high temperatures or expensive equipment. This is known as the 'Utah' experiment. In the 'Utah Experiment' it is claimed that fusion can be caused electrically by making atoms fuse together inside a solid material rather than in very hot gases. The experiment uses Deuterium from sea water. According to the scientists one gallon of sea water could contain the energy of 300,000 gallons of petrol! By April 1989, it is claimed, a sustained fusion reaction for 100 hours had been possible with Palladium and Platinum electrodes in a reaction vessel – a type of test tube.

9

Using energy

For one whole day keep a note of all the ways in which you use manufactured energy. In other words, look at everything you do which is not explained by you, or other people, using muscle power. Do not count walking to school, but do count using the power of the bus engine which carries you a longer distance.

Some schooldays are different from others. On some days you use computers, on others the machines in the craft rooms, whilst a geography lesson involves seeing a film.

Energy, energy and more energy is being used. By the time you put out the light at bedtime (do you have an electric blanket or hot water bottle in the winter?) you may have realized just how much you have used.

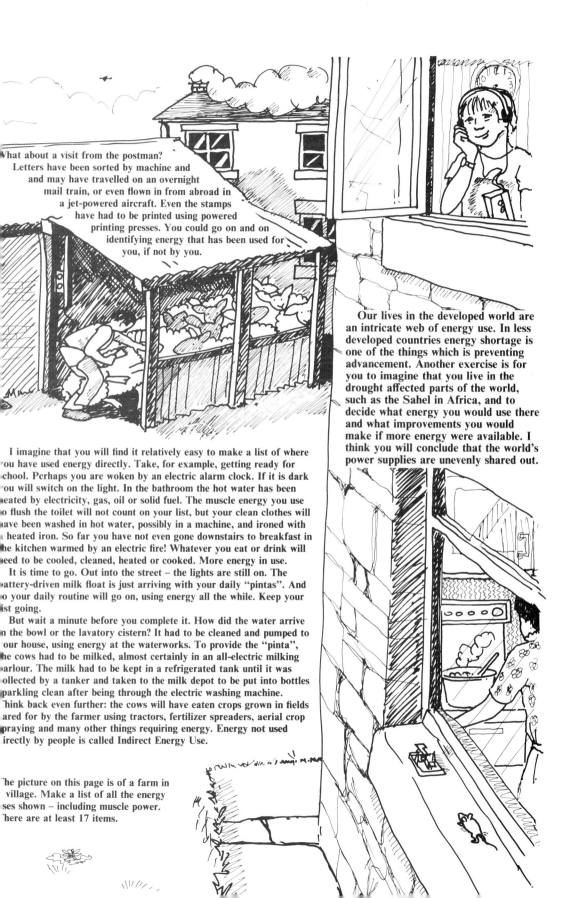

What about a visit from the postman? Letters have been sorted by machine and and may have travelled on an overnight mail train, or even flown in from abroad in a jet-powered aircraft. Even the stamps have had to be printed using powered printing presses. You could go on and on identifying energy that has been used for you, if not by you.

I imagine that you will find it relatively easy to make a list of where you have used energy directly. Take, for example, getting ready for school. Perhaps you are woken by an electric alarm clock. If it is dark you will switch on the light. In the bathroom the hot water has been heated by electricity, gas, oil or solid fuel. The muscle energy you use to flush the toilet will not count on your list, but your clean clothes will have been washed in hot water, possibly in a machine, and ironed with a heated iron. So far you have not even gone downstairs to breakfast in the kitchen warmed by an electric fire! Whatever you eat or drink will need to be cooled, cleaned, heated or cooked. More energy in use.

It is time to go. Out into the street – the lights are still on. The battery-driven milk float is just arriving with your daily "pintas". And so your daily routine will go on, using energy all the while. Keep your list going.

But wait a minute before you complete it. How did the water arrive in the bowl or the lavatory cistern? It had to be cleaned and pumped to your house, using energy at the waterworks. To provide the "pinta", the cows had to be milked, almost certainly in an all-electric milking parlour. The milk had to be kept in a refrigerated tank until it was collected by a tanker and taken to the milk depot to be put into bottles sparkling clean after being through the electric washing machine. Think back even further: the cows will have eaten crops grown in fields cared for by the farmer using tractors, fertilizer spreaders, aerial crop spraying and many other things requiring energy. Energy not used directly by people is called Indirect Energy Use.

The picture on this page is of a farm in a village. Make a list of all the energy uses shown – including muscle power. There are at least 17 items.

Our lives in the developed world are an intricate web of energy use. In less developed countries energy shortage is one of the things which is preventing advancement. Another exercise is for you to imagine that you live in the drought affected parts of the world, such as the Sahel in Africa, and to decide what energy you would use there and what improvements you would make if more energy were available. I think you will conclude that the world's power supplies are unevenly shared out.

Energy around the world

Areas of the world with only one-quarter of the total population possess two-thirds of the available energy sources. In fact, it is more uneven than that, because the United States of America with about 6 per cent (6 out of every 100) people on earth uses 30 per cent of all energy produced. India, for example, has 20 per cent of the world population and uses only 2 per cent of all energy produced.

Why should this be the case? A simple answer is that the geology of the world has concentrated the main known power resources of oil, coal and natural gas in a few places.

North America, Europe, Russia and China have most of the coal. North America, Central America, Europe, Russia and the Middle East have most of the oil and natural gas. The countries with the resources have been able to create industries and to raise the standard of living of their peoples to a high level. They have been able to exploit other power sources such as hydroelectricity, because they have the technology (that is, the machines and the skills to use them) and the money to build dams and provide turbines and grid systems. Countries such as the USA, the USSR, Japan and others including the United Kingdom have therefore become known as the DEVELOPED WORLD. Those countries which do not have enough energy, and use less of the world's resources, are often called the DEVELOPING WORLD.

In these latter areas particularly in the countries of South East Asia and Africa, most of the energy which is used is for growing and cooking food. The power source is mainly firewood. Countries which suffer energy shortages are often those which have long periods without rain. Droughts mean a lack of tree growth and crop failures followed by hunger and starvation. The recent terrible sufferings of the Ethiopian population are only partly relieved by money from charities such as Band Aid and from Western governments.

With few machines, the Ethiopians need a large family to farm the land. Poor standards of education and a low understanding of modern medical practices, including birth control, mean that the energy-poor countries have rapidly increasing numbers of people. The energy crisis is just one of many problems which lead to a rapid increase of world population, often known as the Population Explosion, the greatest conservation problem of the present time.

Possession of energy reserves gives a country political and economic power. The leading fossil fuel in the world is oil. Almost one-half of the energy used in the world for transport, industry, heating, electricity and so on comes from oil.

Energy uses and reserves around the world. *The symbols on the map show the amount of fossil fuel produced and fuelwood consumed in the eight regions of the world. MTOE = million tonnes of oil equivalent. This is a measurement of energy, based on the energy obtained from using 1 million tonnes of oil.*

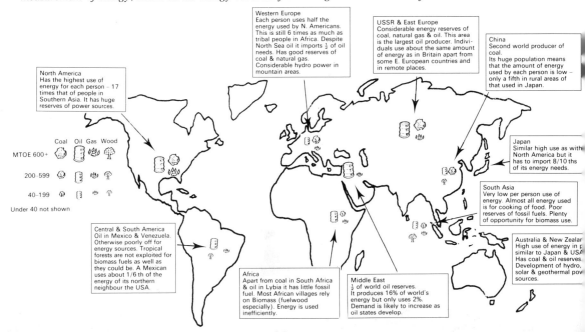

Western Europe
Each person uses half the energy used by N. Americans. This is still 6 times as much as tribal people in Africa. Despite North Sea oil it imports ½ of oil needs. Has good reserves of coal & natural gas. Considerable hydro power in mountain areas.

USSR & East Europe
Considerable energy reserves of coal, natural gas & oil. This area is the largest oil producer. Individuals use about the same amount of energy as in Britain apart from some E. European countries and in remote places.

China
Second world producer of coal.
Its huge population means that the amount of energy used by each person is low – only a fifth in rural areas of that used in Japan.

North America
Has the highest use of energy for each person – 17 times that of people in Southern Asia. It has huge reserves of power sources.

Japan
Similar high use as with North America but it has to import 8/10 of its energy needs.

Coal Oil Gas Wood
MTOE 600+

200-599

40-199

Under 40 not shown

South Asia
Very low per person use of energy. Almost all energy used is for cooking of food. Poor reserves of fossil fuels. Plenty of opportunity for biomass use.

Central & South America
Oil in Mexico & Venezuela. Otherwise poorly off for energy sources. Tropical forests are not exploited for biomass fuels as well as they could be. A Mexican uses about 1/6 of the energy of its northern neighbour the USA.

Australia & New Zealand
High use of energy in p similar to Japan & USA. Has coal & oil reserves. Development of hydro, solar & geothermal pow sources.

Africa
Apart from coal in South Africa & oil in Lybia it has little fossil fuel. Most African villages rely on Biomass (fuelwood especially). Energy is used inefficiently.

Middle East
½ of world oil reserves. It produces 16% of world's energy but only uses 2%. Demand is likely to increase as oil states develop.

A combined coal mine and power station, Rugeley, Staffordshire. *The coal is mined and taken direct into the power station.*

OPEC is the Organization of Petroleum Exporting Countries and it is controlled mainly by countries of the Middle East, such as Saudi Arabia. Even though many of the developed countries have their own oil resources, their demand for oil energy is so great that they are also the main oil-importing countries of the world. In 1973, for many reasons, OPEC increased greatly the price of oil and so created an international money crisis. Since then, the fluctuating price of oil has caused many of the commercial problems of the developed world, including some of the difficulties of the UK's economy. The discovery and use of oil from the North Sea has helped to stave off problems in this country. Even so, Western Europe and the USA import much of their supplies of oil.

The world supply of oil is not limitless. Despite new finds, reserves are running out and more and more it will become a raw material for the chemical industry (most plastics come from oil) rather than a fuel to be burnt. Coal, on the other hand, exists in huge reserves. It is estimated that the total coal reserves of the world are 250 times the amount used every year. But this does not mean that its supply is inexhaustible. Most scientists agree that by the year 2400 coal will have become a resource of the past.

Since oil and coal are not sufficient for the future, an alternative energy resource has to be considered: nuclear power. Unfortunately, nuclear (atomic) power is linked in people's minds with atomic weapons of destruction and this leads most people to be apprehensive of nuclear power even for peaceful purposes. Yet those whose job it is to study the energy needs of the world over a long period appear to be convinced that nuclear power, backed by some forms of renewable energy sources, will be the source of energy well into the future.

Still above us the sun shines. Plans to harness its power worldwide may prove to be the answer, with the "colonization" of space

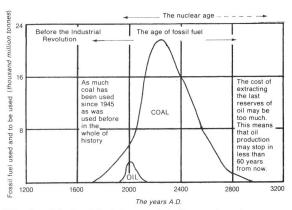

The fossil fuel crisis. *The graph indicates that the amount of oil available is very small compared with coal and in about 200 years oil will run out. What other discoveries may come later? What lies deeper in the earth's crust? What lies on the ocean floors?* (Source: Gaia Atlas of Planet Management)

another factor. Who knows what energy sources have yet to be discovered "out there"?

Will all of this come in time to offset the gross inequality of our present-day energy uses? What might happen in a hundred years' time is of little comfort to those searching now for wood for the fire and food for the family.

An oil tanker ablaze in the Persian Gulf. The SS Norman Atlantic *on fire after Iranian attack, December 6th, 1987.*

Energy conservation

A coal-fired power station.

Pigeons roost on a warm roof. Which house of these two has an insulated attic?

Look at the picture of a coal-fired power station. You must have seen one like it yourself, with one, or possibly two or three tall, smoking chimneys. Also, several objects which look like giant milk churns gently steaming into the sky, just as your hot bath steams into your bathroom. The steam consists of very small drops of water floating in the air. At the power station the giant "milk churns" are called cooling towers and they cool the steam and hot water which has been used to drive the turbines. The cooled water can then be used again, or returned to the river without causing overheating and so harming the fish.

Think about this process. Fuel is burnt to heat the water to produce steam. The steam is used to generate electricity, but much of the steam is left over and has to be cooled again. All the fuel that was used to produce the spare steam has been wasted and, not only that: those huge cooling towers have had to be built to deal with the steam. They are not a pleasant feature of the view. The steam which they emit often covers the surrounding area like a man-made cloud. People who live in the Ironbridge valley near Telford in Shropshire will tell you that sometimes the sun is completely shaded by the steam plume from the local power station.

Look at the picture of pigeons on the roof of a house. Do you notice that they are all clustered on one part? Can you guess why this is? The photograph was taken on a cold day, so I think that the birds were keeping themselves comfortable on the warmest roof through which a lot of

Heat losses from a typical house with conservation of energy protection.
(a) Double glazing prevents heat loss: two sheets of glass at least 6mm apart;
(b) fibreglass roof insulation laid between ceiling joists;
(c) wall insulation injected into the wall cavity between layers of bricks.

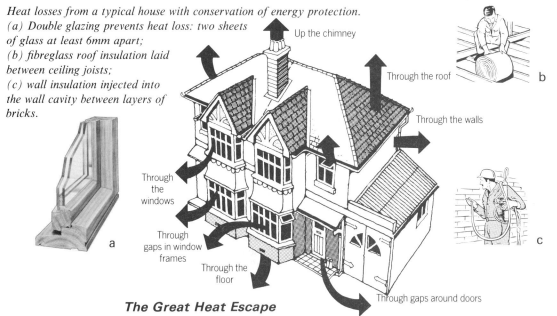

Up the chimney

Through the roof — b

Through the walls

Through the windows

Through gaps in window frames

Through the floor

Through gaps around doors

a

c

The Great Heat Escape

METER READINGS				CD 16/NN	AMOUNT £
PREVIOUS	PRESENT				
		TARIFF D5 - ECONOMY 7			
		STANDING CHARGE			9.20
C001508	C002799	DAY UNITS	1291 AT	5.70P	73.58
C149350	C156818	NIGHT UNITS	7468 AT	1.90P	141.89
			TOTAL AMOUNT NOW DUE FOR PAYMENT £		224.67

PAYMENTS BY POST to MIDLANDS ELECTRICITY BOARD, P.O. BOX No. 18, KINGSWINFORD, WEST MIDLANDS, DY6 8BL. (further advice on methods of payment is given overleaf)

You may have the Economy 7 system of electricity supply in your own home. By having water heating, central storage heating, washing machines and dishwashers on time-controlled switching, it is possible to use night-time electricity "off peak" at the cheaper rate; cheaper because the CEGB knows it will have plenty of electricity to spare during the time when most of us are in bed asleep. For 7 hours (usually 00.30 to 07.30 hours) the cost is cheaper than for the daytime 17 hours, as you can see from the electricity bill.

heat was escaping. The next-door roof was colder. Perhaps that house had no heating on at all, but knowing that people were at home in both houses I think that there is another explanation. The attic below the pigeons had not been insulated and so the house warmth was coming out of the roof slates. The other house had its attic floor covered with a layer of an insulating material. The heat was kept inside the house, and so the roof slates remained cold. The next time it snows, go roof insulation spotting. If you see two houses, one with snow on the roof and the other with the snow melting away, which will be the one without proper insulation, so allowing the heat to escape into the sky?

I have used the word "insulation" two or three times so far. It means blocking something, such as heat, sound or electricity, and preventing it from passing through. In the case of heat energy, some materials allow warmth to pass through them easily – some do not. In other words, some materials are bad insulators and some are good. A layer of air sandwiched between two sheets of glass is a good insulator of warmth. This can be used for windows and is called double glazing. There are advertisements in every local newspaper for double glazing systems. On television, the one named after a very high mountain is well-known. However, the most important measure to take, to prevent heat escaping from a building is to put insulation material below the roof and in the wall cavities. Go into any "Do It Yourself" shop and you will see rolls of thick glass fibre material or polystyrene granules, for use in roofs, floors and walls, to prevent the heat – the expensive-to-produce heat – escaping. Draught excluders, foam rubber tapes, plastic window sheets, and many more items are all designed to keep the heat in and the cold out. ENERGY-SAVING is the name of the game.

If an electric light bulb is left alight with no one using it, the power it is taking is wasted. However, switching off every single unnecessary light in a building will save only a small amount of energy compared with the amount saved by insulating that building to prevent heat loss.

There are times when there is a great demand for electricity. These are called the "peak periods". Charging a higher price for electricity during peak times is one way to persuade people to use less when demand is high. Look at the graph on page 33. Suppose the cost of electricity was made to be much more expensive at any time when demand was at its peak and less expensive when demand dropped? Such a system is known as DIFFERENTIAL PRICING. It would be quite easy for the CEGB to control the costs, and it would be possible to have a complete record made of what had been used, with computerized meters installed in homes and factories. How could the user tell when to use the less expensive power and when not to use the more expensive peak-time power? One idea is for BBC radio to transmit a signal which would indicate the cost of the electricity. This signal would be received by special electric plugs adjusted to switch off an appliance when the electricity became too expensive. Refrigerators, deep freezers and water heaters are appliances which could be signal-controlled to avoid using high-priced peak-time electricity.

What about the terrible waste of heat from those cooling towers? What can be done about that? Turn to the next page and we shall see.

Pollution and energy production

Windscale, Three Mile Island and Chernobyl have one thing in common. They are all the names of nuclear power stations where faults occurred. Only now, more than 30 years later, are we learning how close Britain came to a nuclear disaster when the power generator at Windscale (now called Sellafield) in Cumbria caught fire. The amount of radiation released was small, but even so, many years later one part of the power plant cannot be entered because of the continuing danger.

On March 28th, 1979, a disaster was just averted at the power station on Three Mile Island not far away from Washington, in the USA. A small cloud of radiation escaped.

In 1986 a major radiation cloud did occur from the USSR's Chernobyl nuclear power station. A fire destroyed a third of the power plant and radioactivity released into the atmosphere was carried across Europe at the whim of the blowing winds. Atomic levels in Scandinavia rose almost immediately. It took a little longer for increased radiation to be found in Wales where, more than a year afterwards, some restriction on the sale of sheep still applied.

Unfortunately, using atomic energy to produce electricity has in it the dangers of the spread of deadly radiation, if anything goes wrong. However, we must keep these dangers in proportion. Many nuclear power stations are working without difficulty and the deaths caused directly by the three accidents so far have been 31, all at Chernobyl. I say "directly" and "so far" because one of the worst aspects of a nuclear accident and the leak of radioactivity is that the illnesses and deaths which result may not become apparent for many years, as the cancer symptoms develop slowly.

Non-nuclear power stations are also not free from danger or pollution problems. Coal and oil have to be obtained before they can be used as fuel. In the same month as the Three Mile Island accident happened, 10 coal-miners were killed in a mining accident at Colborn Colliery in Lancashire. Major or minor accidents in coal-mines occur frequently. Ones which involve one or two people are, as often as not, ignored by the news media. For the period 1974–84, the National Coal Board (now British Coal) reported a total of 441 miners killed and an average of 450 injured every year. Similarly, accidents on oil rigs are numerous. If the movements to and from oil fields are included, the list is long. The terrible explosion and fire on the Piper Alpha rig in July 1988, when 167 men perished, was a reminder of the dangers of obtaining oil.

One certain point in favour of nuclear power is that no smoke or gases are emitted. By contrast look at any fossil fuel-fired power station and you will see steam coming from the cooling towers and an exhaust plume from each tall chimney. The steam has some local effect, particularly blotting out sunshine. Since the Clean Air Act was passed in the UK in 1956, the exhaust plumes are usually clean of soot and other carbon bits, known as hydrocarbons. But what of the gases? (If you have read *Acid Rain* in this series you will know all about this problem.) When coal and oil burn they discharge gases, the main ones being carbon dioxide (CO_2), sulphur dioxide and oxides of nitrogen. These gases mix with the moisture in the air to form carbonic, sulphuric or nitric acids, and these acids then affect plants, particularly trees, directly, and increase the acidity of lakes and rivers until eventually all the creatures living in the water are killed.

The Chernobyl nuclear power station after the disaster, May 1986.

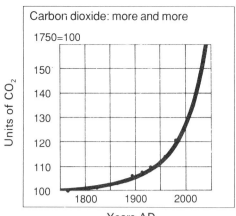

Carbon dioxide: more and more

1750=100

Units of CO_2 (y-axis: 100, 110, 120, 130, 140, 150)

Years AD (x-axis: 1800, 1900, 2000)

If the amount of CO_2 in the atmosphere in the year 1750 AD is taken to have been 100 units, it is now 125. It is predicted that this could rise to 150 in 100 years' time. (Source: *UNEP*)

Carbon dioxide is the gas which provides the bubbles and the fizz in soft drinks. Although there is only a little of the gas in the earth's atmosphere (only about 1 part in a hundred), it is a vital ingredient because of its effect on our climate. As we have seen, about one-third of the incoming solar radiation is reflected back into space (page 8). Some of the heat reflected is absorbed by the CO_2 in the atmosphere and this warms the surface of our globe. Since the great upsurge in the burning of fossil fuel in about 1850, at the time of the Industrial Revolution, the concentration of carbon dioxide in the air has increased by something like 30 per cent. Every year the world burns 5 thousand million tonnes of fossil fuel. The burning of forests adds to the amount of carbon dioxide the world creates and, in addition, the decrease in the number of trees makes the problem worse, because trees do the job of absorbing CO_2. The increase of CO_2 in the atmosphere is the main cause at present of the Greenhouse Effect which is causing a warming of the world's atmosphere. If the amount of CO_2 doubles by the year 2060, as seems likely, the Greenhouse Effect will result in average temperatures increasing by 1°C at the equator, 3°C in the temperate latitudes where we live, and even more at the poles. The ice of the Arctic and Antarctic will melt a little more and the waters of the oceans will warm and expand. The level of the sea will rise, and a rise of only half a metre would cause many coastal areas to be flooded including London and New York. At the same time, drastic changes in the climate will mean that in our northern latitudes the winters would be shorter and wetter and the summers longer and drier. Sub-tropical regions would become even drier than they now are and tropical ones even wetter. Perhaps some of the freak weather conditions of recent times – drought in Ethiopia, a hurricane in the south of England – could already be an indication of the Greenhouse Effect.

The Greenhouse Effect
Heat from the sun enters the greenhouse and the glass prevents the escape of much of this heat. It reflects it back into the greenhouse (see page 21). This is why the inside warms up on a sunny day. In a similar way, when heat from the sun reaches the earth's surface, much of the long-wave radiation is prevented from escaping back into space by various gases in the atmosphere which absorb the heat. If there was no atmosphere, or only a little, the world would be a very cold place.

How greenhouse gases increase the earth's temperature. *By the year 2030 AD, the average temperature may rise by between $1\frac{1}{2}$°C and $4\frac{1}{2}$°C.* (Source: *UNEP*)

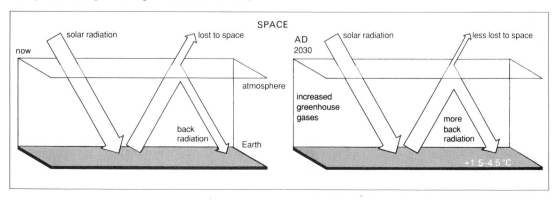

Combined heat and power

Hot air balloon at Disney world where everything is done to use energy efficiently.

In Walt Disney's World in Florida, USA, everything is done to entertain you – and to keep you pleasantly warm or cool all the while. One thing is certain: a lot of electricity is used to keep all the attractions working and well-lit, and the environment really comfortable. The Central Energy Plant generates and sends electricity, hot water, chilled water and compressed air all around Walt Disney's World. This is a "total energy system" in which the equipment uses waste heat to produce hot water and removes heat to produce chilled water. The system saves a great deal of energy, without spoiling the comfort of people or the efficiency of the equipment.

A system of this kind, which provides electric power and uses the waste heat to provide hot water for household purposes and for central heating, is called a COMBINED HEAT AND POWER SYSTEM (CHP). Such systems take the maximum benefit from the fuel used.

In Walt Disney's World the electricity and hot water produced are used entirely by the park. In other cases the power produced can be fed into a national grid system as we have in the United Kingdom. The heat can then be used to supply central heating and hot water for homes and businesses in what is known as a DISTRICT HEATING SCHEME (DHS). It can be sold to factories for industrial purposes and other heat

The Midlands Electricity Board's CHP station at Fort Dunlop, Birmingham. *Heat is planned for the Dunlop tyre factory, known as Fort Dunlop building, beside the CHP plant. Electricity is fed into the national grid system. Two diesel engines and two coal-fired boilers provide 24 MW of electricity and the equivalent of 23 MW of heat. The plant is 78% efficient.*

If you travel on the M6 you can see Fort Dunlop clearly and beside it the tall silver-coloured chimney of the CHP station.

Energy efficiency diagram to illustrate the fact

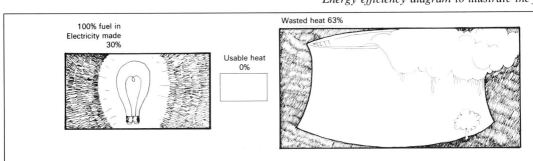

100% fuel in
Electricity made
30%

Usable heat
0%

Wasted heat 63%

needs. Although the idea for CHP is attractive as a wise use of energy, it has to give value for money. There are four main snags:

1 The high cost of building the electricity-generating station and the pipe network needed to carry the hot water.
2 The loss of 7 per cent of electricity generation (see diagram).
3 The need to sell the heat at a lower cost than if any other fuel were used.
4 The cost of borrowing money to build the technology required.

However, CHP schemes are growing. In Western Europe there were 168 of them in 1986. Now, in the city of Leicester, a consortium (a group of businesses and the local council) is looking at a scheme to buy and modify the local Central Electricity Generating Board gas turbine power station. The idea is to use the heat it produces for a heating and hot water scheme especially for that part of Leicester bordering the river Soar and the Grand Union Canal. Two independent networks will be established, one distributing steam and the other hot water.

CHP systems will have other beneficial effects besides providing a more efficient energy system. Many more jobs will be created in manufacturing pipes, laying them underground, fitting meters, constructing the necessary buildings and maintaining the system. Here is a list of some other advantages for CHP. Can you think of more?

Lower fuel bills.
More people will benefit from cheaper warmth, especially the elderly.
There is no longer a need to own a domestic water heater and maintain it.
Only heat used is paid for.
The value of a property in a DHS is higher than the value of one outside.

Heavily insulated pipes being buried for a district heating scheme.

Factories with their own waste heat can sell it to the CHP scheme.
There will be less air pollution from one central well-controlled heat generator.

You must also consider the adverse effects. CHP may create jobs, but fewer domestic boilers and less domestic maintenance will mean fewer people employed with these. If the DHS increases property values, it also means that property is more expensive to buy. Nothing is straightforward or simple. I explained to you that all of the steam from power station cooling towers is wasted heat. It would be a splendid source of heat for a DHS. But can you think of a major difficulty? If you think about where you see the largest power stations, you will realize that they are usually in the middle of the countryside, many miles from a town. So much pipe work would therefore be needed to set up a DHS, that the whole thing would be far too expensive, even though from a conservation point of view, it would be worth it to save our fossil fuel reserves. Nevertheless, there are some large power stations beside built-up areas. Rugeley, in Staffordshire, is one example.

CHP station cuts down waste by nearly a half.

100% fuel in
Electricity made 37%

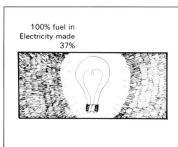

Usable heat 55%

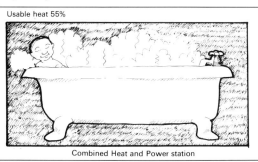

Combined Heat and Power station

Waste heat 15%

Solar energy

The sun was shining down from a clear blue sky despite the fact that it was early in February, still mid-winter in England. I even had to move from my corner seat on the train, which was taking me from Wolverhampton to Oxford, because the sun's rays through the glass were bright and hot. The powerful diesel oil electric engine was pulling the coaches along at high speed, passing the huge Didcot power station on the right-hand side. "What a pity," I thought. "Oil being burnt at the front, coal being burnt on the right, and to the left the sun's energy pouring down neglected by the power engineers." Surely if I had found it too hot to sit in the path of the few rays which reached me, there was enough solar power around to move the train and make electricity?

There is no doubt that it will be possible to use the sun's power in this way in the future, but so far our technology is limited to fairly small uses of solar power and to research experiments. In my corner seat I was being warmed directly; no special aparatus was needed to use the power of the sun. This is an example of PASSIVE SOLAR ENERGY. The railway carriage itself was getting hotter; it had become a SOLAR COLLECTOR. To use the sun's power to make the train move or the power station work would need some machinery or technical equipment. The sun's energy would need to be changed, to

Parking a car on a sunny day can lead to problems. When the driver returns, the inside of the car can be like a hot oven. The seats are hot and the steering wheel too hot to handle. Leaving the windows open is to invite theft. Apart from covering the seats and wheel with a blanket and covering the windscreen with a cloth, there is not much that can be done. The car has become a passive collector of solar energy. Even if it is cold outside, the inside of the car will be warm from the trapped heat of the bright sunshine.

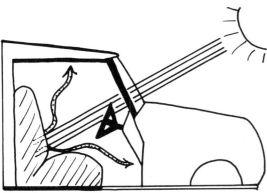

If you wish to see solar energy at work (and many other energy systems as well), go to the Centre for Alternative Technology sited in a disused slate quarry in mid-Wales near to Machynlleth. School groups are made very welcome. It really is an exciting place to visit.

make power production possible. This is called ACTIVE SOLAR ENERGY.

Solar power is most likely to be useful where the sun shines for more time than it does in the northern part of Europe. Cloudy conditions hamper the use of direct solar energy, although even when clouds obscure the sun, the ultra-violet rays still reach the earth's surface and can be collected for energy supply use. But many of the uses made of solar power do need direct sunshine. If you go to Crete or Cyprus or to other islands and lands of the Mediterranean Sea where the sun shines during most days, you will see simple solar equipment on nearly every roof, supplying the hot water needs of that home.

Passive solar energy
Occasionally the weather in Britain is hot enough to fry eggs on the pavement, a trick which newspaper reporters like to play, to create headlines for their paper during a heat wave. In

A building with a passive solar wall, at the Centre for Alternative Technology.

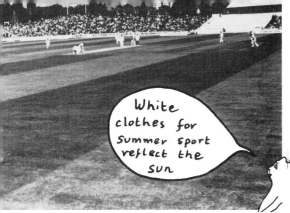

anything else inside. A lot of it is reflected back into the air as long-wave heat radiation. This will not pass back through the glass. Instead it is trapped inside the greenhouse and heats up the air. The greenhouse acts as a solar collector. At night, with no extra sunshine entering the greenhouse, the heat escapes as the glass absorbs the warmth and radiates it back into space.

sunny countries the stone walls are often too hot to sit on, and the paths around a swimming pool too hot for walking barefoot. In all of these cases the sun has heated the surface directly. This is passive solar energy at work. In sunny climates passive solar energy is used in the case of houses which have solar walls, to provide warmth in the bright but cool part of the year, and to enable cooling of the inside to take place in the very hot seasons. Henry's house (page 26) is like this. It is near Albuquerque in New Mexico, USA, where the sun shines on most days. To be effective, a solar wall must face the sun. New Mexico is in the northern part of the world, and so sunshine comes from the south. Henry's house faces that direction. If it were in New Zealand, in the southern hemisphere, it would need to be facing north. In New Mexico, and further south in Mexico itself, walls are often built of mud bricks called adobe. These walls readily absorb the heat and warm up the house. In northern India, south-facing, heavy-weight, dark-coloured walls of tightly packed earth blocks act as solar heat stores. Heat-absorbing walls are called TROMBE walls. Quite often nowadays the outsides of these walls are covered with polythene sheeting or glass which traps the heat inside.

A greenhouse is another example of passive solar heating at work. The short-wave light radiation of the sun passes through the glass walls. Much of it is absorbed by the plants and

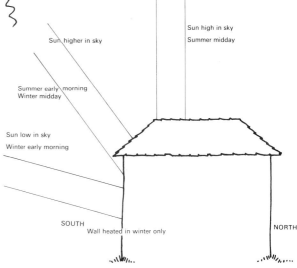

The effect of the angle of the sun on a house in the northern hemisphere.

Solar collectors do three things:

1 Let sunlight in through the glass. (Plastic works in the same way.)
2 Absorb the sunlight and change it into heat.
3 Trap most of the heat inside.

Even in our country solar heating is possible. In St Georges School, Wallasey, across the river Mersey from Liverpool, one whole wall is designed as a passive solar energy collector. It gains half of the heat needed to warm the building. As at Terraset (page 24), warmth is also derived from the body heat of pupils and from the heat given off by the overhead lighting.

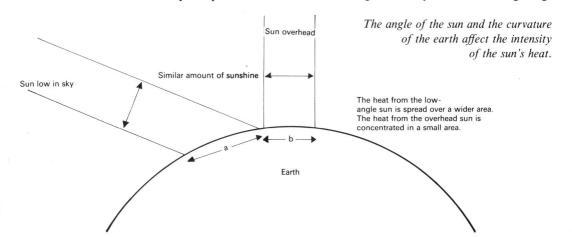

The angle of the sun and the curvature of the earth affect the intensity of the sun's heat.

The heat from the low-angle sun is spread over a wider area. The heat from the overhead sun is concentrated in a small area.

Solar energy (active)

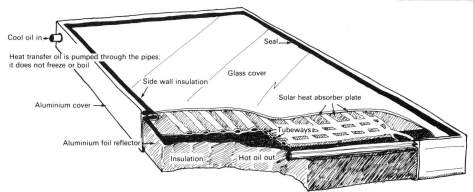

Cool oil in ►

Heat transfer oil is pumped through the pipes; it does not freeze or boil

Seal

Glass cover

Side wall insulation

Aluminium cover →

Solar heat absorber plate

Aluminium foil reflector

Tubeways

Insulation

Hot oil out

This builder's sign hanging on the wall of a house in Eastbourne indicated that work was going on inside to install a solar heating system using solar collecting panels. The sunshine is sufficient to provide some solar heating. A typical design of a solar panel is shown in the diagram. The panel absorbs the energy from the sun and transforms it into heat which can then be moved as a hot liquid, along pipes, to where it is needed. The collectors are usually mounted on a south-facing roof which absorbs heat, even if the sun is not shining directly on it. The panels are examples of an ACTIVE solar system. In houses with such systems in the United Kingdom, the heat produced is added to the usual central heating provided by fuel-fired installations. In sunnier parts of the world, virtually every house has a solar panel and water tank on the roof and this alone gives an almost never-ending supply of hot water. Solar panels – usually in a whole banked array – are also useful for providing heat for swimming pools.

Creating heat from solar energy is relatively simple; creating electricity is another matter. The solar (or photo-voltaic) cell is one answer which uses the high technology of the silicon chip, invented mainly through the development of space travel. Solar cells absorb sunlight and turn it directly into electricity, by the photo-voltaic process. In this process, particles of light called PHOTONS strike layers of semi-conducting material. This causes ELECTRONS to be knocked loose, to flow into connecting wires and become a current of electricity. This sort of

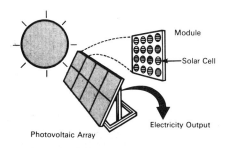

Module

Solar Cell

Photovoltaic Array

Electricity Output

Electricity (DC) production from a photovoltaic array, Solar Energy Research Institute, Colorado, USA (top left);
A solar-powered refrigerator and a solar panel (top right);
A solar cell array, Sandia, New Mexico, USA (far left);
A single solar silicon cell is small enough to be held in the hand (left).

electricity is known as Direct Current (DC). The materials in the cells generate electricity – without moving, making a noise or giving off polluting gases.

Solar cells are already in use for powering small objects such as watches and calculators, as well as larger items such as the electrical appliances in a home. They have the great advantage of being completely mobile. The electricity which comes from power stations through the national grid is called Alternating Current. To feed the power from solar cells into the national grid, it is necessary to change it from DC to AC. This is not difficult, but a nuisance nonetheless. The biggest problem with solar cells is that they are expensive to make. Much research is being put into making them cheaper. One possible answer is to cover glass with thin films of silicon, rather than using silicon completely on its own.

Other systems for creating electricity from solar energy involve using the heat of the sun to make steam to turn turbines and so generate electricity in the usual manner.

Solar ponds make use of the peculiar fact that in salt-water ponds and lakes the water is saltier at the bottom, and heats up more than the less salty water at the surface. It appears that the radiations from the sun pass through the less salty top layers of water into the heavily salted water deeper down. Here the sun's heat is absorbed. If the mixing of the top and bottom layers can be prevented (by using other chemicals), then there is a situation with cool water at the top and very hot water at the bottom. Solar ponds are made about 2 metres deep and need to cover a large area to provide enough useful hot water to be used for power generation. Experiments with solar pond electricity generation are particularly interesting in Israel, especially in the very salty Dead Sea area. It is unlikely that solar ponds will be useful anywhere in the world in latitudes more than 40° from the equator. Outside these latitudes the sun is never directly overhead for very long and so its rays are reflected rather than absorbed into the pond.

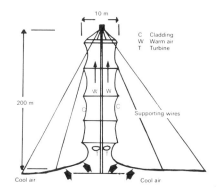

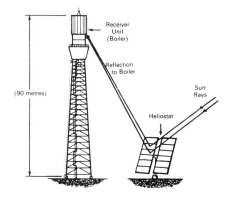

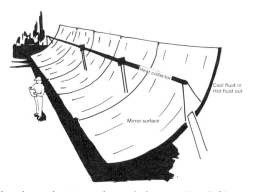

Solar thermal units: a thermal chimney (top left), *a thermal tower (* top right*), a thermal trough* (above) *and a thermal dish* (right). *The sun's rays strike the mirror surfaces and are reflected onto the solar heat collector. The whole apparatus moves to follow the sun.*

Terraset

Terra is the word for earth in Latin. This is the school badge.

People and energy
That is the Terraset story

The heating system at work in school.

The earth-covered school

How would you like to go to school like a mole? In other words, go underground for your lessons? The 900 children of Reston in Virginia, USA, not far from Washington, who attend Terraset Elementary School, do just that. At least they go into a modern building which is constructed into the side of a hill and so, apart from the entrance, is under the ground. Why?

The answer is to save energy! The soil and the rock act as insulators, stopping heat from the inside escaping. Solar panels bring in the power

Grass grows on the roof of Terraset. The various boxes, pipes and sheds are all part of the system for making sure that fresh air is supplied to the interior. The solar panels and collectors are in the background.

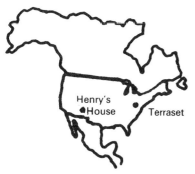

The locations of Terraset and Henry's house in the USA.

for evening meetings, the interior cools down. Before the children come in to school the following day, the heat exchanger and fans work in reverse. The stored warmth is taken from the hot-water tanks and passed back into the school. The whole operation is controlled automatically by three computers.

The school also has some electric heaters which can be switched on using the public power supply. When I visited the school it had been open for five years and this reserve heat supply had not been used at all. Of course, artificial light is needed all of the while. Otherwise Terraset is just like any other school.

of the sun. But most of the heat comes from the children themselves.

During the day the children move about and get hot – just as you do in your school. At Terraset, the heat cannot escape, for there are no windows. It is extracted by cooling fans and passed on to a heat exchanger (see page 39). The heat warms up tanks of water. After the children have gone, and after the school has been used

The ground is an excellent insulator. Caves and cellars stay at a nearly constant temperature. This is one of the reasons why wine is stored in cellars, where the heat will not vary very much.

Above the entrance to Terraset. Looking down from the roadway above the open courtyard, which leads to the entrance lobby. Above the building are the mass arrays of solar panels and collectors. There are 2,750 metres (about 1¾ miles) of collection pipes.

Henry's house

Henry's House from the south.
Can you see the various features of
the solar energy system in the
other pictures?

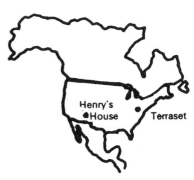

The locations of Terraset and Henry's house in the USA.

*The front roof with the Clerestory
behind it. Air circulation fans,
large solar panels called 'Big Fins' and the solar cell
panel.*

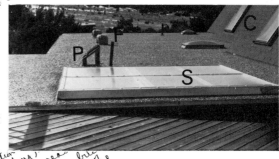

Sandia Park, New Mexico is located on the Sandia Mountains at approximately 7,000 ft. The summer temp ranges from 75 – 85° F and the winter is about 40° – 50° F. The sunshine in New Mexico is present about 250 – 300 days per year. Rainfall about 12 – 15 inches during the year. Basically, a desert climate. Ideal for solar use.

Our home a 2700 square feet wood frame, one story was planned for solar energy use. Our two acre lot is unobstructed on the south to take advantage of the low level during the winter months.

home was constructed with heavy insulation – walls + 12" fiberglass batts on the roofing. Sunlight transmitted thru the glass area – windows + the upper clerestory to the brick walls + the north side of the house. The amount of radiation that on the home is radiated out accurately by the architect or in the structure is important determine the speed of loss (heat) double glaze to prevent heat loss up at night this winter has been the temp inside never went below there were clouds + little or no sunshine, stable temp. Of course to deal with cloudy days we have a woodstove electric baseboard heat (which we have never used)

*The photovoltaic
cell panel*

26

LETTER FROM *HENRY*

Sandia Park, New Mexico, is located on the eastern slopes of the Sandia Mountains at approximately 7000 feet (2100 m) above sea level. The summer temp ranges from 70°–85°F (20–30°C) and the winter temp can get as low as 15° below 0°F (−25°C). Day time temp in the winter is usually between 40–50°F (5–10°C). The sunshine in New Mexico is present on average 250–300 days per year. Rainfall about 12–15 inches (300–800mm) during the year. Basically a desert climate. Ideal for solar energy use. Our home, a 2700 sq ft (250 sq m), wood frame, one story structure was planned for solar energy use.

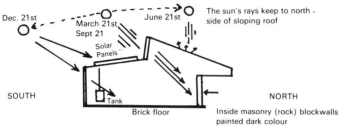

In winter months, the sun's rays are transmitted thru the glass areas on the south side lower walls & the upper clerestory to the brick flooring & block walls on the north side of the house. The heat captures by the mass in the home is radiated out into the rooms after sunset. The insulation of the structure is important in the total design. It will determine the speed of loss (heat). All glass surfaces are double glazed to prevent heat loss. Although the outside temperature at night this winter has been below freezing for months, the temperature inside never went below 65°F (18°C). During the days when there were clouds the home maintained its stable temperature. Of course, to deal with temperatures below 70°F (21°C) we have a woodstove back up as well as electric heat (which we have never used).

On the south facing roof we have a solar panel. Large fins painted black on the ouside receive the sun's rays. On the underside copper pipes run to a water tank. A photo voltaic panel provides energy to a water pump which circulates hot water thru the system. The tank is also equipped with a back up electric system. There is also a great amount of open space in the house which allows full circulation of the warm air.

Wall with glass in front of it

C Clerestory
F Fans
P Photovoltaic Cell
S Solar Panel
T Trombe Wall

The solar system at Henry's House

Henry's House gains 60/65% of its energy needs from the sun. If he had to pay for fuel and electricity to replace the solar power it would cost him $1500 (£830) a year to heat the house and warm the water instead of the $600 (£330) he pays now. The USA and New Mexico governments allowed Henry to pay less tax in order to pay for his solar house. Unfortunately they no longer give tax help for solar energy.

Geothermal energy

Mount Vesuvius near Naples in Italy. Volcanoes erupt to spew out flaming lava and hot gases – evidence of the intense heat inside the earth.

HOT ROCK – it sounds like a pop group! In fact, it is an alternative source of power or heat. Its scientific name is GEOTHERMAL ENERGY. Rock deep down under our feet is heated by radioactivity and by chemical effects so that, on average, the temperature increases by 25°C for every kilometre of depth. If the rocks at higher levels prevent the heat escaping (we say that they have a poor thermal conductivity), then the deep rock will become very hot. If this extra heat is fairly near to the surface it is possible for engineers to drill down, as with an oil well, and tap this dry rock heat by pouring cold water down one hole and drawing it out hot from another. The two boreholes side by side are called a doublet. In some parts of the world it is not even necessary to drill. Steam and hot water actually emerge from the ground, often in great spurts called GEYSERS, for example in Iceland and New Zealand. These are used to supply hot water for central heating or directly. In Reykjavik, the capital of Iceland, 99 per cent of homes use natural hot water. About two-thirds of the whole of Iceland uses the thermal water for domestic purposes, and few homes built within the last 40 years have chimneys, for they have no need for fires or stoves. Steam provides the power for electricity generation. There are hydro-thermal power stations in Japan, Iceland,

Italy, the USSR, New Zealand, El Salvador, Mexico, the Philippines and California, USA.

For the dry rocks to be really useful there needs to be a large thermal gradient. This just means that the temperatures must become hotter quickly as the drill hole goes deeper. Like the gradient of a hill, the thermal gradient can be gentle or steep. The steeper it is, as far as the amount of heat is concerned, the better. Crystalline rocks, which do not let water flow through them easily, are the best heat-providers. Granite is a good example. It is an impermeable rock: it will not let water through. So how does the water get through from one borehole to the other? This is where the skill of the mining engineer comes in. It is necessary to make the boreholes follow a path into the ground which

Rosemanowes Quarry near Falmouth, Cornwall. An experimental Hot Dry Rock (HDR) project is being run by the Camborne School of Mining, with government funding. The first idea was to sink two parallel wells to a depth of 2 km. Explosives were used to crack the rocks at depth and water was pumped in to prise open the fractures. Unfortunately, the granite rock broke up all over the place and three-quarters of the water pumped in was lost. A third well had to be drilled, to intercept the cracked area. A sticky gel, similar to wallpaper paste, was pumped down in vast quantities. This sealed many of the cracks and cut down the water loss to a quarter. At 2 km the rocks are not hot enough for electricity to be made, so it is planned to drill down to 6 km. This project is planned to be complete by 1995. In March 1988 the government announced that it was putting another £8.15 million into the Rosmanowes project.

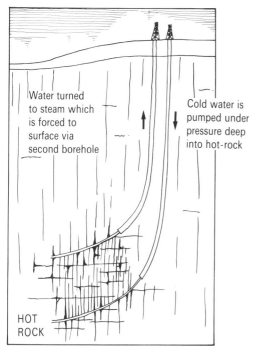

A cross section through a doublet Geothermal Borehole System. The engineers fracture the rocks between the ends of the boreholes by using explosives and forcing water into the rocks at very high pressure. The rock fills with water to become a vast underground hot-water "sponge".

Water turned to steam which is forced to surface via second borehole

Cold water is pumped under pressure deep into hot-rock

HOT ROCK

looks like a letter J if viewed from the side. Between the ends of the two holes the engineer causes the rock to fracture, so that water will flow along the cracks which have been made. This is done by using explosives and pressurized water.

Unfortunately, water will also escape along fractures in the rock which go further down into the earth. If too much leaks away it is not possible to get enough back again to the surface.

Geothermal heat can be used to generate electric energy, either by using the steam which emerges to turn a turbine or by having a heat exchange unit (see page 39) to extract the heat from the hot water and use it to create steam from another water supply. One reason for not using the groundwater direct is that it is often too full of mineral deposits, which would damage electrical equipment.

To be useful for electricity generation, the rocks need to have a temperature of at least 200°C. This is twice the temperature of boiling water. A hot sauna bathhouse is normally about 30°C. If you have ever been into one you will be able to judge just how hot the geothermal water is. Lower temperatures of 85°C would be suitable for providing hot water for district heating. It may be possible to drill a group of five doublets to provide about 33MW of electric energy. Four times as many doublets will generate 132MW, but because the size of the system has increased, with hardly any increase in running expenses, the actual cost of each unit of electricity made will be much less.

There are certain difficulties with obtaining dry rock geothermal energy. Although only an area of about 50 square metres is required for the completed well heads at the surface, at least a hundred times that amount of land is needed during construction. Access roads will need to be built and pipelines laid to carry the hot water to the power station. Locally the noise of drilling may be a nuisance as, too, could artificial earthquakes triggered by the cracking of the rocks underground. To make the effort and the money spent worthwhile, a planned lifetime of 25 years is the least that must be expected of the geothermal installation.

The grand aim must be to make it possible to tap the heat of the inside of the earth at any place, even where easy-to-get-at hot rocks do not exist. It will be necessary to drill down about 3 to 9 kms and even more, in order to encounter usable heat. The drilling itself is not a problem, for with ordinary rotary drilling it is possible, even now, to reach a depth as great as 15 km. But it is expensive, so that a cheaper method for penetrating the earth needs to be found. Rock-fracturing techniques will need to be improved, and a way found of keeping very deep artificial cracks open as passages for the water supply.

A geothermal electricity power station at Geyser Field, California, uses the steam and hot water which escape to the earth's surface.

Wind energy

A windmill at Avoncroft Museum.

"An area of low-pressure is moving slowly across the British Isles. Winds will be from the south-west, reaching storm force at times".

How many times have you heard this sort of remark during a TV or radio weather forecast? Why is the mention of "pressure" important and what "pressure" is it? Quite simply, it is the weight of the air above our heads pressing down on to us. Like other ingredients of the weather, air pressure can be measured, in this case by a barometer. This gives a reading in "bars", the measure for air pressure. In practice, the measurement is taken in millibars, 1/1000ths of a bar. Normal pressure is 1000 millibars (mbs). As you go up into the sky, air pressure gets less, which is why astronauts wear pressurized space suits and why the cabin of a high-flying aircraft is pressurized. Without these precautions, at sufficient height, people would burst!

Air pressure varies mainly as a result of the heating of the earth by the sun. Where the surface is hottest, air rises, leaving a lower pressure at ground level. Where the earth is cool, the air falls, causing high pressure. If pressure is high in one place and low in another the air will move from high to low; in other words, the wind is blowing. Differences in heating between land and sea mean pressure variations. These give us sea breezes blowing from sea to land during the day and from land to sea at night. Coastal areas are thus the windiest, ideal for making electric power by means of the wind turning the blades of wind turbines.

Windmills have been used for centuries to turn machinery. Pumps worked by wind sails have been used to drain the water from the land in the English fenlands and in the Dutch polders. Have you read the book *Don Quixote* (pronounced Key-oh-ty)? In it Quixote thought that the wind sails in Spain were the enemy, and so he attacked them. In a wind turbine for making electricity, the wind blows and turns the sails which nowadays are shaped like the wings for a glider. The sails turn the turbines and the

Erecting a wind turbine. In November 1987 a 3 MW wind turbine was officially "opened" on top of the 90-metre-high Burgar Hill in the Orkney Islands, north of the Scottish coast. It cost £12 million and joined other experimental wind turbines on the same site. The blades of the new machine are 60 m wide from tip to tip. This means that 7 double-decker buses could stand in a line beside the blades and still have some room left over at each end. The turbines generate electricity for Orkney homes. In spite of their large size, 700 such machines will be needed to match the output of the proposed new Sizewell "B" nuclear power station.

Nevertheless, it was announced on March 23rd, 1988, that the CEGB, with £30 million of government grant, will build 3 wind farms each consisting of 25 turbines. The first will be near Launceston in Cornwall. Each farm will require 1 square mile of space. They will be completed by 1990–92. One off-shore wind turbine will be erected also. Each farm will provide electricity for 15,000 people.

An extensive research programme is being carried out in the UK to decide whether wind is a practical source of electricity. This 25-metre-diameter vertical axis wind turbine has been in action at Carmarthen Bay, South Wales, since November 1987. It is based on a design by Dr Musgrove of Reading University. Unlike "normal" wind generators it spins around the column horizontally. When still, the blades look like rugby posts, but when they spin they tilt forward to look like giant arrow heads. One great advantage of this design is that it does not need to face into the wind in order to get the full benefit from it.

turbines make electricity. What do you guess is the basic trouble with using wind as a source for power?

Japanese cargo ship with rigid sails. They save 15% of fuel consumption.

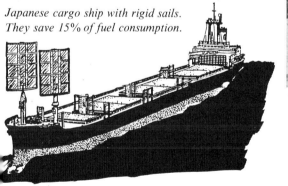

Right! The wind does not blow all the time, even though in some places it does blow fairly regularly. The wind speed must be over 25 mph for the sails of bigger machines to turn well enough to produce electricity. Too much wind is bad as well. Strong gales, such as the terrible hurricane which blew across Southern England on 15 October 1987, could damage the machinery by making the sails turn too fast – the supporting column might collapse or a blade break off. The blades need to be locked in position in extra-strong wind conditions. Most small wind-powered generators of about 4KW have an automatic switch-off at wind speeds over 34 mph.

Normally, each wind turbine produces about 60KW of power, although larger 1000KW machines are being manufactured. It is therefore necessary to have a lot of wind turbines together in order to generate sufficient power to be of real use. A collection of wind turbines is called a Wind Farm (see the picture on the front cover of this book). Although each wind machine is a marvel of engineering, they are not the most attractive of objects. In order to catch the most wind they have to be sited in full view, spoiling the look of the open countryside. They cannot be screened with trees, for instance, for these

The turbine-driven Falcon. *It has a wind sail which points head to the wind no matter which way the boat itself is travelling. The greatest speed is still achieved when the boat is moving with the wind behind it, but even into the wind it can travel quickly.*

would stop the full force of the wind reaching the turbines. They can be sited out to sea, on islands or man-made structures. But the electricity has to be transported by power line and the bigger the distance between the electricity generator and where it is needed, the more expensive and difficult it is. If the wind turbines are not too far out of the way, the power can be tapped fairly easily into the electricity grid system already existing.

The real difficulty with wind power is that the total amount of electricity which can be generated is very small compared with the output of a conventional power station. (To generate 1,000 MW – the size of a nuclear plant – would need a land area of 200 square miles covered with turbines.) Therefore, relying wholly on wind machines is not a sensible possibility, except for smaller, local projects.

Water power

Niagara Falls: the Canadian Horseshoe Falls.
I have been lucky enough to stand on the deck of the Maid of the Mist, *a boat which sails right up to the foot of the water crashing down over Niagara Falls on the Canadian/USA border. Hour after hour, day after day, year after year, the river cascades over the Niagara Cliff. If the skipper had made a mistake, the falling water would have crushed the vessel to matchwood. Can you spot it in the picture?*

The Hoover Dam, near Las Vegas, USA. *This huge dam (it was called the Boulder Dam originally) blocks the water of the Colorado River and forms Lake Mead.*

The strength of falling water is immense. If this enormous force is "captured", it can be made to turn a turbine and so generate electric energy – hydro-electric power – exactly as is done, for instance, at Niagara Falls. Wherever there is a natural waterfall there is the possibility of building a power station. It has been estimated that 25 per cent of the world's electricity comes from hydro schemes, and that this represents about 5 per cent of energy needs. Hydro power is the most practicable of all forms of renewable energy for, except for the occasional drought, the water keeps on flowing.

Hydro schemes do not have to be of a massive size as with Niagara. In fact, as we shall see with the Aswan example, large projects often cause severe problems. In China there are about 90,000 small hydro-electric power plants, most of them built in the last 20 years. Between them they produce 5,000 MW of energy. Most of the electricity is used locally for supplying hospitals, schools and rural industries. In Zambia, the Zambezi river is another mighty waterway. On one remote farm beside the river, small water-wheels are being used to pump water around the fields to supply the crops; an efficient irrigation scheme. It has been so successful at providing electric energy as well that there is now a massive plan to install 10,000 small waterwheels in

the area to provide both irrigation and electricity.

All rivers flow downhill, but usually with too small a drop for a hydro scheme without some other construction. That is why DAMS are necessary. Quite simply, a dam blocks the flow of the water and causes an artificial lake to fill up behind it. This is called a RESERVOIR. When it is full, the surface of the water above the dam is much higher than that in front of it, and if the water were permitted to spill over the top, it would make a man-made Niagara. However, instead, the water is drawn off into large pipes which carry it down and into the power station built below. Here the water rushes through a turbine, turning it and the electric generator, before returning to the river further downstream. If there is a natural lake on high land, it may be possible to tap into it and to bring the water downhill to a power generator.

Often the best location for a hydro station is where the fast-flowing river has reached the lower land. Building a dam and creating a lake inevitably involves land being flooded, sometimes even whole villages. The power station itself, and particularly the grid lines and pylons, can be unsightly. If the need for power is so great, the land, farms and villages may have to be lost. This can cause much distress and argument. As a conservationist, which way would you vote?

Power stations can be well-hidden, even underground, as in the case of Kielder near Newcastle on Tyne. The transmission cables

The Machine Hall at Dinorwig. The heart of a mountain has been tunnelled away to make space for the turbines and other machinery. Two natural lakes, Llyn Peris at the bottom and Marchlyn Mawr at the top, have been linked with tunnels through which water can flow at 92,400 gallons EVERY SECOND. On its way it passes through the turbines which turn the generators. These same turbines act as pumps to reverse the flow when required.

The power house is built in a man-made cavern, 2 football pitches long and half a pitch wide, with a ceiling higher than a 16-storey tower block. Dinorwig produces 1,740 MW. In an emergency, it can make 1,320 MW in just 10 seconds.

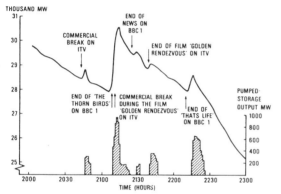

The Thorn Birds *set a record for the biggest electricity demand at the end of a single television programme. On the evening of Sunday, January 22nd, 1984, shortly after 9 pm, there was a sudden increase in demand of 2,600 MW. Why do you think power demand* increased *when the programme was over? The shaded areas of the graph show the vital part played by the pumped storage power stations (Ffestiniog and Dinorwig).*

called, uses the spare night-time electricity available from other power stations. Stopping coal- or oil-fired power stations and then starting them up again is expensive and wasteful. It is better to keep them going all of the time, using their spare electricity for pumped storage. This happens at the remarkable installation at Dinorwig, near Mount Snowdon in North Wales. Unless you know what signs to look for, there is nothing to be seen. Basically, pumped storage power stations are used at times of peak demand, to back up the power generated elsewhere. They take at night and give out during the day. They are examples of the use of Potential Energy. Look back to page 4 if you have forgotten what this is.

Aswan High Dam

The main intention of the Aswan High Dam, built between the years 1960 and 1970, was to provide water for irrigating the fields along the banks of the Lower Nile. It was known that the formation of Lake Nasser, the reservoir behind the dam, would submerge many important archaeological sites and the town of Wadi Haifa. What was not known was that as well as blocking the water the dam would prevent the silt going downstream. Now the reservoir is gradually filling up and the silt is not available to "fertilize" the fields.

For the first time, the *fellahins* (local small farmers) are having to buy artificial fertilizer. Fish food carried in the silt fails to reach the Mediterranean Sea. With less food there are fewer fish, and the fishing industry of the Nile delta has been virtually wiped out.

taking the electricity to join the national overhead grid system have been put underground for a great enough distance to avoid the scenery being spoilt. The artificial lake, Kielder Water, has become a delightful countryside feature and a resource for leisure activities, such as boating, angling and water skiing.

Once used, the water has gone downstream and is lost. If, instead, the water could be sent back up, it could be used over and over again. To pump it to the top takes more energy; in fact, it usually takes more electricity than the power station can produce. However, it is worthwhile doing, since PUMPED STORAGE, as it is

The restless waves

Although it appears from waves that the water is moving forward, it is actually going up and down. It is the wave ripple which is moving forward, caused by the wind blowing on the water surface. Watch a seagull sitting on the sea and you will see that it stays in the same position as a wave passes, merely moving up and down.

> "All expenditure on research into wave energy should cease in 1986 and the technology involved should be relegated to the 'reject' or 'long shot' category."

This was the disappointing conclusion of the Advisory Council on Research and Development for Fuel and Power – ACORD for short. Fortunately it also said that "awareness of programmes elsewhere and of new ideas should be maintained". The Department of Energy accepted these findings but within two years changed its mind and allocated nearly £$\frac{1}{4}$ million to build Britain's first wave power station on the Hebridean island of Islay (pronounced Eye-la).

Remote islands require costly electricity generators, or costly, difficult-to-install electricity supply cables which have to run under the sea. Although the wave power station on Islay will produce less expensive electricity than other wave methods, it will still be more expensive than electricity produced at a conventional power station.

An Oscillating Water Column. Norway has been making OWC wave power since 1985.

The proposed equipment for Islay is known technically as an Oscillating Water Column, where the pressure of air in a hollow column drives a generator. As the waves cause the water to rise inside the cylinder, air is forced out of the top. This turns an air turbine. As the water falls, air is sucked in. By using a clever piece of equipment, known as a rectifier, this falling water also turns the same turbine. A generator produces electricity.

There have been several other ideas for harnessing the power of the waves:

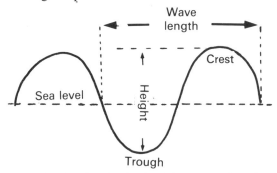

Waves break when the depth of the water is less than half the height of the wave.

1 The Oscillating Vane or Duck

Cone-like objects, held together in a long line by a central spine, bob up and down (oscillate), moved by the waves. They are linked to a rotary pump, which helps to turn an electricity generator. The idea came from an engineer named Stephen Salter, and the term "Duck" was used because some people thought that the bobbing movement was similar to that of a duck nodding its head up and down to the water.

2 The Raft

Three large floating rafts are linked but each one moves independently. Between one raft and the next there is a cylinder containing a piston surrounded by fluid. This is called a hydraulic ram. The waves move the rafts, the rafts move the rams, the pistons move the fluid – and this makes a turbine turn and so creates electric power.

3 The Rectifier Lock

Imagine a long construction built up from the sea bed with a series of very big letter-box-type openings. Set this in the path of the waves. The top of a wave will force open the "letter-box" flap and the water will flow in. As the water falls to the trough of the wave, the water inside the lock will flow out again at a lower level. During its journey it will pass through a turbine and generate electricity.

4 The Clam

This consists of a ring of about a dozen air bags which are squeezed by the movement of the waves. As each bag is pushed, air is forced out of it. The air drives a turbine and this leads on to electricity generation.

5 The Tapchan (TAPping the CHANnel)

In a way this is similar to a tidal barrage, but on a much smaller scale. In a suitable rocky inlet of the sea the wave will rush in and overflow into a reservoir. When the wave retreats, the sea water will spill out again and drive a turbine in a method similar to that used in a normal hydro-electric scheme.

To be realistic, wave power seems to be impractical for making large amounts of electricity. It has been estimated that to produce 2,000MW of power, as from a small power station, would need a length of Ducks stretching from Edinburgh to King's Lynn (find them in your atlas). However, for fairly local use, especially in remote coastal areas, there may well be a place for wave power.

One very good thing in favour of wave power is that waves are at their strongest when the winter weather is the roughest – precisely the time when most electric power is needed.

Perhaps, after all, ACORD got it wrong!

The Tapchan power plant near Bergen in Norway was opened in 1985. The wave (at least 75 cm high) flows in along the channel and fills the reservoir. It is claimed that power stations up to 300 MW can be built using this method. A Wave-collecting channel, B Reservoir (11,000 sq.m.), C Power station (350 KW), D Sea

Some difficulties with wave power

The electricity produced has to be moved from the wave unit to the user. This means difficult electrical links on the unit and cable connection to the shore.

Floating objects may interfere with ships and fishing.

The power installations may disturb fish shoals

Waves reflected back out to sea from the power equipment may cause rougher water for small boats.

Some advantages with wave power

The wave energy barriers may calm the waters between them and the shore, and so reduce coastal erosion, especially in the case of islands.

As waves will batter the moving parts, a lot of necessary maintenance work will create many jobs.

Unlike wind generators, wave energy equipment will not spoil the view.

Wave energy can be used with desalination plants (which take the salt out of sea water to produce drinking water) in what is known as a *total energy package*, providing fresh water and electricity at the same time.

Tidal energy

The tide clock
at Saundersfoot,
South Wales.

The tide clock
at Saundersfoot,
South Wales.

Beachy Head, Eastbourne. The same place, morning and afternoon. Tide in, tide out.

At the seaside the sea may be a long way from the shore at one time of the day and yet right up against the promenade at another. We say that the "tide is out" or the "tide is in", as the case may be. The regular fall and rise of the water level, as the diagram shows, has the effect of making the sea move down the beach, away from the shore, at one time, and back up the shore $6\frac{1}{4}$ hours later. It is the gravitational pull of the sun and the moon on the earth and its oceans which causes the tides to occur. How far the water goes in and out depends on the difference in rise and fall of the tide and, more especially, on the steepness of the sea bed. The amount of rise and fall depends on the time of the month and the time of the year and on the shape of the shoreline. In a river estuary (where it joins the sea) – for instance, the River Severn estuary – the rising tide is trapped in a narrowing funnel shape, which makes the water rise even more than along the straight coastline nearby.

If the high-tide water in the estuary could be held back and released later, when the water elsewhere was low, it would have to drop a considerable height. The falling water could be sent through a turbine to generate electric power, as in a hydro-electric system. This is called Tidal Power. The rising water can be trapped behind a barrier across the estuary known as a Tidal Barrage. In the UK the estuaries of the Severn and the Mersey, Morecombe Bay, and the Wash have been investigated as suitable tidal power locations. Some places, including Southampton, have double tides which might be an added advantage for tidal power.

At the present time (1989) there are six working tidal power stations. Three are in China, one is in Russia, one is in Canada in the Bay of Fundy, and one is in France at the Rance River estuary near St Malo. The electricity generated has to be taken away. In the UK the grid system could easily take in electricity generated by a tidal barrage. If major available tidal power sources in the UK were harnessed, up to 20 per cent of the present demand for electricity could be met. Perhaps there would be no need for several controversial nuclear power stations if full use were made of the tides.

Tidal races

In some areas of sea between islands, or between the mainland and an island, the change of tide causes a fast flow of water to take place. These are known as tidal races. They are well-known to seamen, for they are extremely dangerous to shipping and can be very rough indeed. It might be possible to "harness' their power for tidal electricity purposes. The Pentland Firth along the north of the Scottish coast is one location of a tidal race.

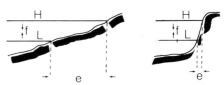

The steepness of the shore affects how much beach is exposed at low tide. Where the shoreline slopes gently, the amount of beach exposed (e) is large. Where the shoreline is steep, the amount of beach exposed (e) is small, even though the fall (f) between high (H) and low (L) tide is the same.

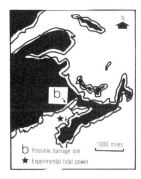

Possible barrage site
★ Experimental tidal power
1000 miles

Canada. *The Bay of Fundy has the largest tidal range in the world. Between high and low tide it can be 14 metres (at least twice the height of a normal house). A test scheme is already in operation within the bay. If it works well, other barrages may be considered.*

France. *The success of the small Rance estuary barrage has led to investigations into cutting off a large area of the coast just to the east of Jersey, one of the Channel Islands. The lines* **bbb** *mark possible sites for the barriers. The Rance barrage is 700 m long, has 24 10 MW turbines. It was opened in 1966.* →

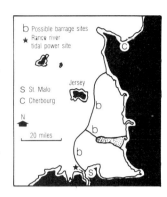

b Possible barrage sites
★ Rance river tidal power site
S St. Malo
C Cherbourg
Jersey
20 miles

The Mersey Estuary.
Thought has been given to placing barrages at either 1 or 2. The demand for power in nearby Liverpool is enormous.

The Severn Barrage

The idea of a barrage across the estuary of the River Severn has been discussed for many years. Various linking points have been suggested: most lately from a point near Cardiff, on the Welsh side, to Weston-super-Mare on the English coast. This scheme is being investigated by the Severn Tidal Power Group, which is made up of six companies, the CEGB and the Department of Energy. The Severn estuary's tidal range of 11 metres is the second highest in the world. It has been estimated that 13 thousand million kilowatt hours of electric current could be generated every year – enough for 3½ million homes. This is about 5% of the annual amount needed in the UK. Others claim that it could provide as much as 7½%.

Any tidal barrage development would affect a large region around the estuary. During construction, tens of thousands of jobs would be created. It would be possible to incorporate a road or railway link across the barrage and this, in turn, might encourage the siting of factories in the area, providing long-term employment. Access through the barrier would bene-cessary for boats travelling to upstream ports, but these ports would also get the benefit of becoming non-tidal. In other words, the level of the water in the port would remain the same all day and not rise and fall with the tide. While the water held up by the barrage would be saline (salty), it might be possible to construct an area which would contain fresh water coming down from the Severn and so become a reservoir for a local water supply. Building the barrier would need enormous quantities of rock material. Might this be a way of using the waste left over from coal-mining and which now forms large, unsightly heaps in the South Wales countryside?

Creating an alternative and renewable power source by building the barrage would mean that the land on either side of the Severn would be flooded all the while and not just twice a day as at present. The tidal mud flats and marshes would therefore disappear and affect birds, fish, plants and invertebrates.

The Severn Bore a wave of water which rushes upstream, would be lost.

Many other factors need to be assessed. Salmon and eels need to swim to and from the sea. They must be able to reach the rivers Severn, Wye and Usk in order to breed. Ways through the barrage for such fish will need to be provided. What will be the effect on seaside resorts such as Clevedon and Weston-super-Mare? Sewage disposal is involved, as the effluent poured into the river will not be dispersed by the current. The dangers of sea flooding will be replaced by river flooding, and extra drainage measures may be needed in the surrounding farmlands. The list of problems is very long – but the electric energy created by the barrage may be enough to save the building of four or five nuclear power stations.

The companies who built the Thames Barrage so successfully estimate that the cost of the Severn Estuary barrage would be nearly £4 thousand million, that it would take 7 years to construct, and that the cost of electricity generated would be under 3p per KW hour.

Is it worth building the Severn Tidal Barrage? A decision is needed soon.

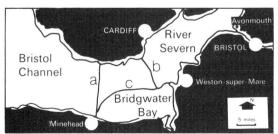

The Severn Estuary. *The tidal range in the estuary can be 11 metres. Many proposals for siting the barrage have been considered. Site* **a** *is the latest;* **b** *might be less difficult to build; and* **c** *could be added later, if* **b** *was successful.*

37

Heat storage and exchange

A very simple *heat exchanger* is used in many buildings to provide hot water. A boiler heats water, which flows through a spiral or coil of copper pipe (E in the diagram) inside a cylinder and back to the boiler for reheating. The hot water in the coil passes its heat to the cold water in the cylinder and this feeds the hot water taps of basins and baths. The coil of pipe is the heat exchanger. Quite often gas showrooms have a cut-away model of a hot water cylinder which shows the heat exchanger. See if there is one in your local showroom.

Most of you will have a refrigerator, and some of you a deep freezer. If not, you will have seen freezers keeping the icecream cold in the newsagent's, or the chickens, meat and gateaux frozen in the frozen food centre. If you listen beside the cabinets, you will hear a motor switching on and off, particularly after the lid has been opened and warmer air has been let in. The motor is part of the system known as a *heat pump*. It is extracting warmth from the air inside the freezer and passing it out into the room, cooling the inside and warming the outside. Most refrigerators, but not all, work like this as well. Heat pumps exchange warmth from one source to another, cooling a freezer or warming the water in a swimming pool, for example.

A heat pump can take heat from water, from soil or from air. Remember Terraset (page 24). In order to work, the pump has to have energy for itself; it requires electricity to make it go. This creates a basic energy problem. Are you able to work out what this is?

Have you realized the problem? It is that a heat pump is only worthwhile for a heating system if you get out more energy than you put in. With a freezer the object is to preserve food. You are using the electric supply for that purpose. It is essential with heating that the electricity used by the heat pump is less than would have been used for direct heating in the first place. Scientists talk about the *Coefficient of Performance (COP)*. This is not the book to explain COP in detail. All I will say is that the COP for an electric fire is 1. The COP for efficient heat pumps varies from 2 to 5. In other words you put in 1KW and get out between 2 and 5KW. With a COP of 3, 1KW in gives 3KW out. This sounds fine and very efficient but we must remember that a lot of energy is lost in producing electricity at the power station and in moving it along the grid lines. These losses must also be taken into account before it is thought that heat pumps are a great way of obtaining "free" energy.

In France, at a place called Creil, in Paris, heat pumps are being used in a district heating scheme to recycle some of the heat from the central heating water. It is at a temperature of about 40°C. The water is divided into two. Three heat pumps (COP = 5) lower the temperature of one part to 7°C, and pass the reclaimed heat on to the other part to raise it to 70°C.

Heat can be stored ready for reuse in bricks or stone or water, as at Terraset. A heat exchange system is needed to release the stored heat. With night storage heaters it is natural radiation of heat into the air which causes the exchange.

Heat pump installation. Warmth extracted from the outside air passes indoors and on through a heat exchanger in a water tank and/or direct to central heating radiators.

Key

E Heat exchange coil
P Heat Pump
B Boiler

R Radiator
T Hot water tank
w Warmth taken from air
h hot water
c cool water

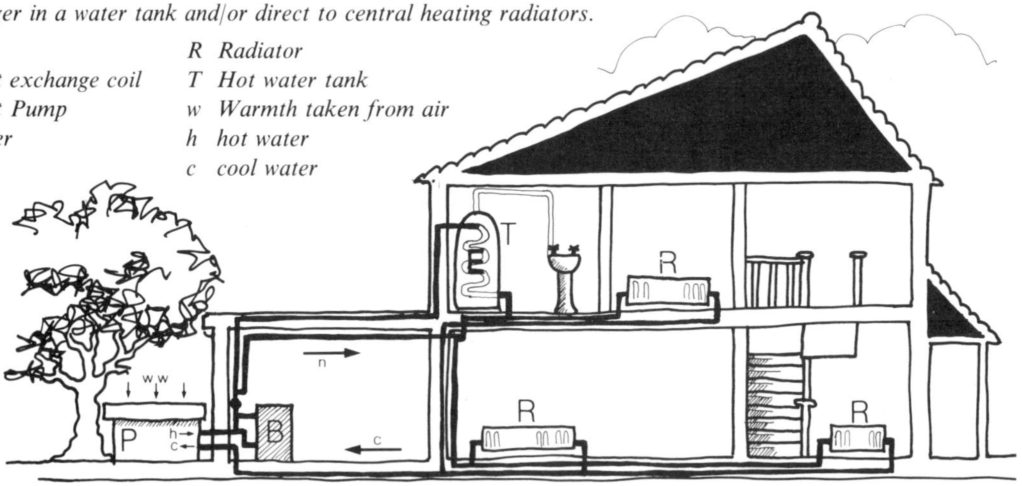

Inside The Heat Pump

Heat Exchanger (the Evaporator) — 1

Compressor

Expansion Control

Heat Exchanger (the Condenser) — 2

Cold in
Water
Hot out

GAS

Evaporated

Liquid

Inside the heat pump. A cold gas is passed through a heat exchanger. It collects heat from the surrounding air. The warmer gas goes into a compressor which puts the gas under greater pressure. This increases the heat of the gas even more. The hot gas goes into heat exchanger 2. Here its warmth is transferred to cold water which becomes hot and moves off into the house or swimming pool heating system. The gas condenses to a liquid because it has lost much of its heat. The liquid passes through an expansion control and back into the first heat exchanger, where it starts its journey all over again.

Storing electricity

Unfortunately, it is not easy to store large amounts of electricity itself. It is possible to store Direct Current in a battery, but Alternating Current, the type of electricity made in power stations for use in homes and businesses, cannot be stored. It is possible to store energy, as we have seen already. For example, storing water behind a dam is one way of having an energy source in reserve (see Dinorwig, page 33). Compressed air can be stored in caves: spare electricity is used to pump it in, and it is allowed to flow out later when needed.

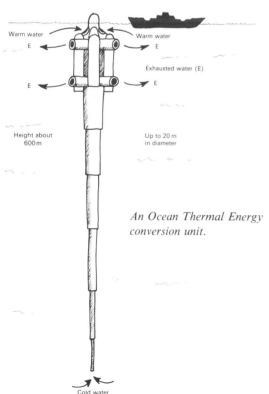

Warm water
Warm water
Exhausted water (E)
E
E
E
E

Height about 600 m

Up to 20 m in diameter

An Ocean Thermal Energy conversion unit.

Cold water

> **Ocean Thermal Energy Conversion (OTEC) – Heat exchange at work**
>
> The oceans of our world are like a huge heat storage tank. OTEC is a system which exploits this fact. In one version of OTEC a fluid with a low boiling point, such as ammonia, is vapourized by the warm surface water, into steam, which drives a turbine to produce electricity. The vapour needs to be condensed back to ammonia fluid. This is done by using very cold sea water, at about 8°C, pumped from deep down. OTEC works best in tropical areas where the surface water is about 28°C. A small OTEC project is working off the coast of Hawaii in the Pacific Ocean. One estimate is that by the year 2000 OTEC could produce as much power as 400,000 barrels of oil. There is no pollution or use of fossil fuel with OTEC.

Large wheels which spin keep going long after they have been given the energy to turn. These are called flywheels. If a power source has a flywheel attachment, any lowering of the power can be smoothed out by the flywheel and the output of electricity continue. This is called an inertial system of energy storage.

Bioenergy – from plants

To us, barbecues, camp fires and bonfires may be pleasant, friendly ways of cooking our food or warming ourselves. But that is not the case for an estimated 3 thousand million people who rely on burning firewood as their only source of heat, apart from burning the dried dung of domestic animals like cows or camels. In the tropical areas of the world, not only is wood the fuel for people to use in their homes, but also governments of certain countries are promoting the introduction and expansion of industry using wood fuel. Such industries include tobacco-curing, tea-drying, brick-making, pottery and tile manufacture, and even the making of steel. Some countries, such as India and the Philippines, hope to produce electricity using steam from wood-fired boilers.

One essential for domestic wood-burning is that the supply is near to the user. For many, the supply of local wood has been exhausted and new trees are not getting the chance to grow. Some people will not have wood for cooking

The collection and transportation of fuelwood in Ethiopia and other developing countries can still be a laborious and time-consuming task.

their food unless more trees are planted. Trees can be grown in plantations, large areas of land growing all the same species of tree. Bioenergy Plantations (their technical name) are a renewable energy source.

Wood can also be turned into charcoal, by smouldering it. Charcoal has about three times the heat energy of wood. Powdered charcoal can even be added to oil, too. However, in the process of making charcoal from wood, half of the actual energy in the wood is lost in the gas and smoke which escape. If these emissions are trapped and then burnt, the heat created can be used. In this case, energy is used more efficiently, air pollution is decreased and fewer trees are required at the start.

Shells from nuts will flare away brightly when thrown on a fire. One factory in California, USA, produces 35,000 tonnes of walnut shells each year. The owners used to crush them into a fine brown powder and sell this as filling for soft toys or as bedding for chickens, or even as an ingredient for making glue. Now, most of it is burnt in the factory's boilers, to make electricity and heat for a CHP (or, as they call it in America, a Cogeneration project). In fact, the walnut-shell burning is so successful that two-thirds of the electricity generated is not needed by the factory itself and is sold to the local power company. All over the world bioenergy is being wasted, although people are beginning to realize just how much of this power is available to them. In the UK, fires and furnaces have been designed to use straw as a fuel. Make a list of all the vegetable matter which could be used as a fuel, not only in the UK but worldwide.

Burning is not the only way to obtain energy from plants. Wood can be turned directly into a gas to fuel engines. Cars propelled by gas are common in Brazil and the Philippines. ETHANOL (wood alcohol) can be produced from wood by a process called HYDROLYSIS.

Another way is to collect fuel directly from living plants. TURPENTINE is a white spirit made from the resin collected from pine trees by tapping (that is, by cutting a slice in the bark and allowing the juice to bleed out). Ponds often have a green, "slimy" covering, especially if the water is still. The green vegetation is known as ALGAE.

Eucalyptus trees (also called gum trees) are a good firewood tree because the wood burns with a strong heat. The trees grow quickly in various soil types, and will grow close together. They coppice well (that is, they grow up again with many shoots when cut down to the base). In Brazil, 11 million of the 38 million cubic metres of fuelwood used for charcoal come from eucalyptus.

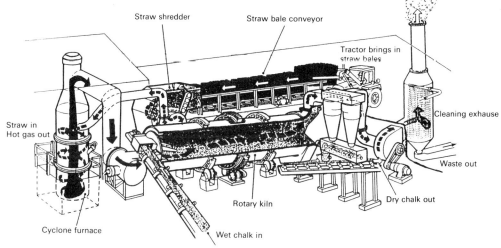

Straw shredder — Straw bale conveyor — Tractor brings in straw bales — Cleaning exhause — Straw in Hot gas out — Waste out — Dry chalk out — Rotary kiln — Cyclone furnace — Wet chalk in

Needham Chalks, *a company in Ipswich, use straw as a fuel in their furnace to dry the chalk dug from their quarry. They use 2,000 tonnes of straw a year, which is easily obtained from the grain-growing farms of East Anglia. Needham Chalks are saving 65% of the fuel they used previously, which means a saving of £80,000 per year. Woburn Abbey is now heated by straw-burning furnaces. In this diagram of a system for drying chalk using straw as a fuel, the kiln and other parts are cut away to show the inside.*

Algae grow easily and quickly, both on fresh water and on the sea, where they are known as MARINE ALGAE. As they grow, they give off hydrogen. Not only does this burn, but the waste left over is harmless water. If the hydrogen could be gathered together, it could be used as a fuel to generate electricity. Experiments are going on at Swansea University to see if it is practicable to "innoculate" large areas of water with algae so that they will quickly spread. An enclosed area will be needed, and it has been estimated that a surface area of 17.5 km² could provide sufficient hydrogen fuel to generate

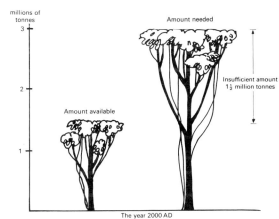

Estimate of the fuelwood supplies in the world by the beginning of the twenty-first century, if nothing is done to alter production.

millions of tonnes — Amount needed — Insufficient amount 1½ million tonnes — Amount available — The year 2000 AD

Cassava roots are fermented to make fuel spirit in SE Asia.

At the present time, 10 cubic metres of wood can be grown each year on 1 hectare. At that rate, 100 million hectares of plantations (200,000,000 football pitches) will need to be added to the natural woodland areas. If the yield could be doubled, only 5 million hectares of land would be required. This could be done by

1 Choosing the best tree species (saman and eucalyptus are very productive).
2 Using good-quality seeds.
3 Raising healthy seedlings.
4 Choosing the best types of tree for the soil.
5 Using good methods of planting.
6 Taking good care of trees after planting (weeding, protecting from animal browsing).

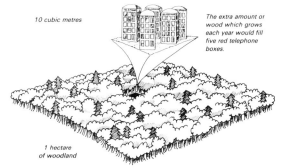

10 cubic metres — The extra amount of wood which grows each year would fill five red telephone boxes. — 1 hectare of woodland

enough electricity for the needs of one million people – enough for a city the size of Swansea itself. Hydrogen, unlike landfill gas, has a high calorific value. In other words, it gives off a lot of heat from a small volume of gas.

Bioenergy – from waste

"WARMER". This is the splendid title for a campaign to turn thrown-away rubbish into heat. Here is what its director, Philip Evemy, had to say at a 1987 conference:

"Warmer's message is simple. Recycle warmth and energy from rubbish. Use the thousands of millions of tonnes of polluted household waste in the world as fuel to produce electricity, steam and hot water for homes, factories, offices and public buildings, thus saving precious fossil fuels, creating employment, and reducing pollution.

*The graph shows how different countries use rubbish or waste to create energy. It shows the total amount of rubbish used (in millions of tonnes) by each country and it shows the percentage of each country's waste which is used for energy. The total amounts of refuse are the most accurate estimates which can be made for the years between 1982 and 1987. (*Source: *Organization for Economic Cooperation and Development: the Warmer Campaign)*

Waste at Perry Barr

The shaded part of each dustbin indicates the amount used for energy creation

On average, depending on how and where you live, *two and a half tonnes* of household waste has the same energy content as *one tonne of coal or 1,200 litres of heating oil*. In Britain, we have been dumping *30 million tonnes* of rubbish a year into holes in the ground – throwing away a fuel resource capable of providing central heating and hot water every year for nearly $2\frac{1}{2}$ million families!"

(*WARMER Bulletin*, September 1987)

If rubbish is not buried, there are two ways by which it can be made to provide heat. The heat can either be used directly to provide warmth or hot water, or indirectly to produce electricity from steam.

Burning rubbish directly

Incineration, to give the process its technical title, is a common way of disposing of waste. At the Perry Barr Refuse Disposal Plant in Birmingham, this method had been used for many years until the closure of the incinerator in 1986. All the rubbish collected from homes and work places in the northern parts of the city was put onto a moving furnace, similar to a "going-up" escalator. No fuel was needed as the waste burnt on its own, assisted by strong blasts of air from giant fans. The rubbish that would not burn was passed under large magnets which removed any iron for recycling. The rest, clinker and ash, was taken away to be used in the foundations of roads and other places. The heat produced was wasted. It went up the chimney with the waste gases to warm the air above and to pollute the atmosphere. The plant is now "mothballed" – in other words, it is preserved for the time when it may be used again without the heat being lost. Another refuse-burning plant at Tyseley in Central Birmingham is still working and wasting heat. Not far away, in Coventry, an incineration plant is not wasting its heat. Every day of the week part of the warmth from the burnt rubbish is transferred to the Peugeot Talbot factory. Next time you see a Peugeot 309 car, just think that its production has been helped by the rubbish thrown away by people living in Coventry. The latest move in Coventry is to

Easiburn is the name given to the RDF factory in Eastbourne, Sussex. Lorries take the pellets to colleges in Eastbourne, Lewes and Hastings and to a nursery garden in Kent as fuel for their heating systems.

RDF pellets. *The large ones are from Easiburn, Eastbourne, and the small ones from France. Pellets have an average calorific value of 6,660 BTU per pound weight (15,500 Kj per Kg). Coal is about 50% higher – 12,520 BTU/lb (29,000 Kj/Kg).*

make the heat from the burning waste produce steam to generate electricity. A similar scheme has been investigated in nearby Wolverhampton, where it is planned to produce electricity at the Crown Street incinerator for sale to the CEGB. In Sheffield, too, a district heating scheme using the warmth from its Bernard Road refuse incinerator is to be extended and eventually used for electricity generation. Indeed, a new power station at Blackburn Meadow is planned, provided that the extension programme is successful.

I hope you have realized that these are examples of CHP schemes such as I described earlier in this book. Unfortunately there are still about 50 refuse incinerators where the heat goes to waste.

Refuse Derived Fuel (RDF)

The other method of providing heat from refuse is to take the rubbish which is brought into the disposal plant and turn it into fuel, which can be burnt in furnaces elsewhere. This is done by breaking the rubbish into small pieces (the pulverization process) and then sorting them into light combustible (able to burn) and heavier incombustible material. Magnets collect the iron from the heavy part and other metals are also collected for recycling. The lightweight rubbish is broken up into even smaller pieces about 50 mm in size. It is then fed into a machine which produces small lumps called crumb. This is dried, using the heat from burning some of the crumb in a Fluidized Bed Incinerator. (This FBI

process is described in *Acid Rain*, another book in this series.) Finally, the dried crumb is passed through a pellet-making machine, where the RDF is made into pieces varying in size from a small to a large sausage. There are now 6 RDF-making plants in the UK, in production or planned for the near future. The one at Eastbourne has been working the longest.

Around the world the practice of wasting waste is being looked at critically, with an eye to recovering material which can be recycled, and using the rest for energy production. By 1997 it is hoped to turn 40 per cent of the rubbish in New York into useful energy. At the present time, about 12 per cent of the 49,000 tonnes of Municipal Solid Waste (MSW) or garbage, as the Americans call refuse, collected daily in that city is used for burning in energy recovery plants. In all of the cities of the USA it is estimated that 460,000 tonnes of MSW are disposed of every day. Until recently, 95 per cent of it was buried in garbage dumps. By 1997 it is said that 8 out of every 10 American cities will have run out of places to dump their rubbish. (In *War on Waste* in this series you can read about the boatload of MSW that no one wanted – it just sailed up and down the east coast of the USA.)

In 1986 98 energy-producing rubbish disposal plants were in operation or being constructed in the USA. Another 35 were planned. Of the total 133, 28 were RDF plants for pellet production. In Japan, 63 energy-from-waste plants were working, and another 10 under construction.

Bioenergy – from biogas

A "Ruston" gas turbine (about 4 m long by 1½ m wide). A similar machine is installed at the Purfleet Board Mills in Essex, using methane gas extracted from the 28-hectare, 36-metre-deep landfill site 3 miles away at Aveley. Thousands of tonnes of rotting refuse from London have been tipped into one of the many former sand, gravel or chalk quarries in this part of Essex. The gas provides one-third of the fuel needed by the factory and the hot exhaust gases from the turbine are fed into a boiler to create steam to drive a "normal" turbine to make more electricity. The waste heat is also used to dry the paper board. What sort of system does this represent? (see page 18).

Gas is produced when material rots away. As it comes from biological action it is known as BIOGAS. I expect you have been aware of that rather odd smell which comes from dustbins and waste dumps. If rubbish is buried, the gas produced is trapped and, just like oil underground, it can be tapped and used. It will burn like the gas we get from coal or from natural gas sources. It is formed by millions of tiny bacteria consuming the degradable waste and giving off gases as they do so. A little over half of the landfill biogas formed is methane, about 40 per cent is carbon dioxide, and some oxygen, nitrogen and other chemicals give it its peculiar smell. A waste tip is really as much a biological reactor as an atomic power station is a nuclear reactor.

The gas will burn and, although it has a lower calorific value than natural gas (it does not give out the same amount of heat), it can be used to heat water and so provide hot water for heating schemes. It can also be used to power gas turbines which in turn will generate electricity. One estimate suggests that all of the landfill gas in Britain's waste tips – if it were properly tapped – would produce a similar amount of heat to that created by burning 5 million tonnes of coal. A most effective, efficient and interesting landfill development exists on the Packington Estate of Lord Aylesford, a few miles from Coventry near to the Birmingham International Airport and the National Exhibition Centre.

At Packington a hill of rubbish is being structured (see diagram) up to a height of 150 metres – about the height of two electricity pylons on top of one another. In other parts of the world hills of rubbish have been built to even greater heights. Already some of the North American sites are so well restored and are of sufficient height as to be made into artificial ski slopes.

Biogas chambers

If anyone you know makes home-made wine or beer you will know that during part of the process gas comes bubbling up from the liquid. A biological process known as *fermentation* is going on. With wine-making the gas is allowed to escape through a special airlock. A similar fermentation process can go on with animal dung, human excreta and any vegetable waste, but in this case the gas is a valuable product as we have already learnt with rubbish tips. Methane is produced in very large air-tight containers which can be called BIOGAS CHAMBERS or DIGESTERS. The methane-rich gas can be used for heating, lighting, electricity generation or for running machinery. In China the production of biogas has become a well-controlled method of waste disposal, particularly for sewage. The method has the effect of recycling resources providing energy and fertilizer, and improving health, because the dangerous bacteria in sewage are killed off in the biogas fermentation process. At the beginning of the 1980s there were thought to be 7 million biogas pits in operation in China. Many other countries, particularly those without advanced power resources, are developing biogas systems. Providing the technical knowledge and money for the equipment is one particularly good and long-term way of helping areas with fuel-wood shortages.

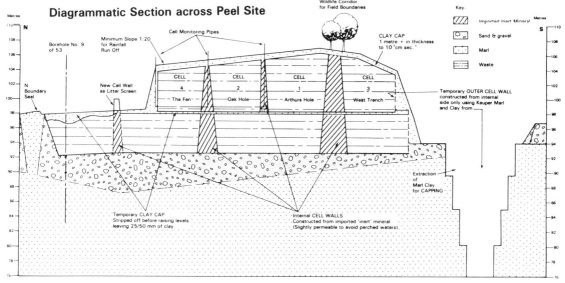

Diagrammatic Section across Peel Site

Wildlife Corridor for Field Boundaries

Key:
- Imported Inert Mineral
- Sand & gravel
- Marl
- Waste

Cell Monitoring Pipes

Borehole No. 9 of 53

Minimum Slope 1:20 for Rainfall Run Off

CLAY CAP 1 metre + in thickness to 10^{-7}cm sec.[-1]

N Boundary Seal

New Cell Wall as Litter Screen

| CELL 4 | CELL 2 | CELL 1 | CELL 3 |

The Fen — Oak Hole — Arthurs Hole — West Trench

Temporary OUTER CELL WALL constructed from internal side only using Keuper Marl and Clay from

Extraction of Marl Clay for CAPPING

Temporary CLAY CAP Stripped off before raising levels leaving 25/50 mm of clay

Internal CELL WALLS Constructed from imported 'inert' mineral (Slightly permeable to avoid perched waters).

The Packington Example. This landfill development site started life as a scheme to fill in holes (technically known as voids) left after sand and gravel had been dug out. Nowadays the holes are full and the rubbish is spread on top of the land surface and formed into a cleverly structured hill. The pipes for extracting the gas are put into the waste tip as it builds up. The natural clay (Keuper Marl) of the site is used to make boxes, or cells, to contain the compressed waste. Cells can have a surface area of between one and four hectares (about 2 to 8 football pitches) with walls 3 to 4 metres high. The clay cap is at least a metre thick, built with a slope of 1 in 20, in order to allow for a quick run-off of surface water. Once a cell is capped, it is covered with soil and sown with grass and clover to be used for grazing. Packington can deal with 4,000 tonnes of domestic, industrial, commercial and construction waste every day. It actually receives between 400,000 and 600,000 tonnes each year. Eventually the gas produced will be used to produce 3.7 MW of electricity which will be fed into the grid system. (Reproduced from The key to safe tipping – Packington Estate Enterprises Ltd – PEEL)

Subsidence (the sinking of the ground as the waste below shrinks in volume) is much less at PEEL than elsewhere. At Packington the rubbish is compressed by large waste scrapers with heavy spiked wheels, into 1.2 tonnes per cubic metre compared with the average 0.6 tonnes per cu m elsewhere. This leads to a 3% subsidence at Packington, compared with 17.5% at other sites.

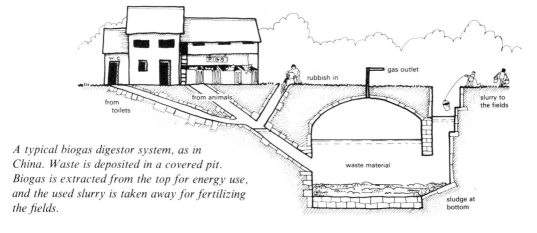

A typical biogas digestor system, as in China. Waste is deposited in a covered pit. Biogas is extracted from the top for energy use, and the used slurry is taken away for fertilizing the fields.

from toilets

from animals

rubbish in

gas outlet

slurry to the fields

waste material

sludge at bottom

Glossary

Acid Rain:	Rain or other precipitation with a low pH brought about by sulphur dioxide and nitrogen oxide gas emissions from chimneys and car exhausts.
Atom:	The smallest particle of an element which has the chemical properties of that element.
Barrage:	A barrier across a river.
Bioenergy:	Energy produced by organic material such as wood and rubbish.
Biogas:	A flammable gas produced by anaerobic (without oxygen) fermentation. In chemical composition it is a mixture of some 60–70 per cent methane, with carbon dioxide and traces of other gases.
Biomass:	All types of animal and plant material which can be converted into energy.
Chain reaction:	A continuous atom splitting process, releasing energy and emitting more neutrons.
Chemical energy:	Energy stored in a substance owing to its chemical composition, usually released by burning.
Conduction:	A method by which heat is transferred from one body to another. Other methods are **Convection** and **Radiation**
Conserving energy:	Using various techniques to prevent energy waste.
Core:	The heart of a nuclear reactor containing the fuel.
Crude oil:	Petroleum liquid obtained directly from the oil well.
Deuterium:	An isotope of hydrogen whose nucleus contains one neutron and one proton. Sometimes known as "heavy hydrogen".
Diffuse radiation or insolation:	Radiation from the sun which arrives on earth as a result of the scattering of direct solar radiation by water vapour and other particles in various layers of the atmosphere. It is also known as indirect radiation.
Direct radiation or insolation:	Radiation from the sun which reaches the earth's surface without being scattered.
Ebb and flow:	The going out and coming in of the tide.
Energy:	The capacity to do work.
Energy conversion:	The transformation of energy from one form to another form.
Finite resource:	A power source which will eventually be completely used.
Fuel cell:	An electrochemical device for converting chemical energy directly into electricity energy without combustion.
Generator:	A machine for making electricity.
Geothermal aquifier:	A source of useful hot water found at depth.
Geyser:	A spurt of hot water and steam from the ground in volcanic areas.
Global radiation:	The sum of direct solar radiation and diffuse radiation. An alternative definition is radiation at the earth's surface from both sun and sky.
Groundwater:	Water which has soaked into the ground.
Heat:	A form of energy. It can be transferred from a body at a higher temperature to another body at a lower temperature as a result of the temperature difference between two bodies.
Hydrocarbon:	A chemical compound containing only carbon and hydrogen. Hydrocarbons form the main part of the fossil fuels.
Isotopes:	The name given to chemically similar atoms with the same number of protons but with different numbers of neutrons.
Kinetic energy::	Energy which is used directly.
Methane:	The lightest of the hydrocarbon gases (CH_4). It is the major constituent of natural gas and is also formed from the decomposition of organic material.
Natural gas:	Naturally occurring gaseous mixtures. The main gas is methane, with smaller quantities of butanes, ethane, hexanes, pentanes and propane.
Nuclear reactor:	A device for producing heat that can be used for generating electricity through a controlled fission chain reaction.
Organization of Petroleum Exporting Countries (OPEC):	A group of thirteen countries which hold between them approximately 65 per cent of the world's proven oil reserves.
Peat:	The first stage in the formation of coal. Hand-cut peat has a high moisture content.

Petroleum:	A general term describing a wide range of hydrocarbons from natural gases, oils, petrol, bitumen and solid paraffin waxes.
Photosynthesis:	The process by which plants convert the power of the sun into energy.
Plasma:	A gaseous mixture of electrically neutral, positive and negative ions at very high temperatures.
Potential energy:	Energy possessed by a body but not yet used.
Power:	The rate of work or the rate at which any energy conversion takes place.
Power tower or solar tower:	A tall tower, perhaps 500 m high, positioned to collect reflected direct solar radiation from an array of heliostats.
Primary energy:	Energy available in any fossil fuel such as oil or coal before it has been processed or transmitted.
Renewable energy:	Energy from sources that are continuous or that can replenish themselves naturally.
Satellite:	Machine in space orbit around the earth.
Silicon:	The commonest element which makes up the earth. Sand, quartz and glass are made of silicon.
Sun:	A star at the centre of our solar system.
Synfuel:	A high quality fuel, usually gas or oil, derived from one of the fossil fuels.
Tide:	The rise and fall of the sea because of the "pull" of the sun and moon.
Turbine:	A machine which is turned by a power source and which itself turns an electricity generator.
Water cycle:	The system by which water evaporates from seas and rivers to form clouds and rain which falls back to earth again.

Useful addresses

British Wind Energy Association, 4 Hamilton Place, London, W1V 08Q

CEGB, Sudbury House, 15 Newgate Street, London, EC1A 7AU

Combined Heat and Power Association, Bedford House, Stafford Road, Caterham, Surrey, CR3 6JA

Electricity Council, 30 Millbank, London, SW1P 4RD

Friends of the Earth, 26–28 Underwood Street, London, N1 7JQ

National Society for Clean Air, 136 North Street, Brighton, BN1 1RG

Solar Energy Research Institute, 1617 Cole Boulevard, Golden, Colorado 80401, USA

United Nations Environmental Programme (UNEP), PO Box 30052, Nairobi, Kenya
(Publishes information papers called UNEP Briefs. Number 1 deals with the Greenhouse Effect and holes in the Ozone Layer.)

Warmer Campaign, 83 Mount Ephraim, Tunbridge Wells, N6 8BS

Book list

A Chinese Biogas Manual, Edited by Ariane van Buren, Intermediate Technology Publications, 1979 (ISBN 0 903031 65 5)

Acid Rain, Philip Neal, Dryad Press, 1985 (ISBN 0 85219 784 5 1988)

Alternative Energy Sources, R. H. Taylor, Adam Hilger (ISBN 0 85274 476 5)

Energy, National Geographic, Special Report, February 1981

Energy around the world, J. C. McVeigh, Pergamon Press, 1984 (ISBN 0 08 031649)

Energy from the Waves, David Ross, Pergamon, 1979 (ISBN 0 08 023271)

Energy without end, M. Flood, Friends of the Earth, (ISBN 0905066 465)

Geothermal Energy, H. C. H. Armstead, Spon (ISBN 0 419 12220 6)

Handbook of Electricity Supply Statistics, Electricity Council (annually) (ISBN 0 85188 114 9)

The GAIA Atlas of Planet Management, Edited by Norman Myers, Pan Books (ISBN 0 330 28491 6 1985)

Wind Energy, Kovarik, Piper and Hurst, Domus Books, 1979 (ISBN 0 89196 034)

Index